GW00776768

Cooking For Life

A Total Vegetarian, Wheat Free and Gluten Free Cooking Experience

Stephanie Bergsma

cookingforlifecookbook@gmail.com

Published April 2013

Copyright © 2013 Stephanie Bergsma
All rights reserved.
ISBN: 1484134621
ISBN-13: 978-1484134627

Table of Contents:

Desserts Continued:

Miscellaneous

Dedication:

This book is lovingly dedicated to the memory of my mother-in-law, Christine Bergsma. Christine loved to cook for others and was known by many for her delicious, one-of-a-kind meals. But more importantly, she was known for her hospitality, smile, kind words and making sure no one ever left the table hungry. She welcomed anyone and everyone into her home and around the family dinner table, no matter how last-minute their arrival was. Everyone felt like family when they were around Christine and she always spoke positively about others. Christine lost a short but courageous battle with cancer in October 2012 and she is greatly missed by all who knew her. She was and continues to be an inspiration as to how we should always treat others.

"Be not forgetful to entertain strangers: for thereby some have entertained angels unawares."
Hebrews 13:2

"Inasmuch as ye have done it unto one of the least of these my brethren, ye have done it unto me." Matthew 25:40

Foreword:

If experiencing great health for a lifetime is on your bucket list of things to do, then "Cooking For Life – A Total Vegetarian, Wheat Free and Gluten Free Cooking Experience" is a cookbook you will definitely want to use often. Stephanie Bergsma has taken her love of cooking and baking and fashioned them into a way of life that has helped her and her family overcome various health issues and can help you attain abundant, vibrant health as well.

In a time when healthcare costs are spiraling out of control, and food sensitivities and health conditions such as diabetes, hypertension, high cholesterol, and cancers are on the rise, cooking healthfully for ourselves is an essential and easy way to take charge of our own health. And, a plant-based way of eating is definitely the way to go! It's so neat that God's Word identifies this, and scientific research clearly corroborates it!

When people hear the words "plant-based", many immediately jump to the conclusion that boring salads are what they'll be eating. Stephanie proves them wrong with such delectable recipes as Stamppot, Chickpea "Tuna" Salad, Savory Coconut Edamame, Quinoa and Black Beans, and Carob Toffee Dream Bars. Believe me, these are in no way boring! The 80+ recipes in "Cooking For Life" are going to make your taste buds so happy, put pep in your step, and set the stage for your increased well-being and optimal health.

I couldn't write this Foreword without trying at least one recipe to test the "delicious-quotient". So, I tested the Quinoa and Black Beans recipe and then, being the sweet-loving gal that I am, I just had to try the Frozen Carob Peanut Butter Pie. All I can say is, "Oh, my stars!" They were both so delicious!

What a loving God, to have provided us a plethora of plant foods to tickle our fancy and provide superior nutrition all at the same time. He wants us to be in total health, emotionally, physically, and spiritually, and He has sprinkled His promises of good health throughout the Bible. I'm so glad Stephanie answered God's call to share her knowledge, first-hand experience, and expertise with us. With added extras like sample menus, helpful tips, and a pantry check list, Stephanie has created an excellent, well-rounded resource to assist you in your quest for life-long healthy living. Friends, you're going to love "Cooking For Life"!

Bev Miller, BASc, Registered Dietitian
Host of "Live Healthy Now!" on Rogers TV
http://www.theveggieliciousdietitian.blogspot.ca

About the Author:

Stephanie Bergsma was born and raised in the Ottawa Valley in the village of Alice, just outside of Pembroke, Ontario. Cooking and baking was something that she always had a love for, even as a small child. She spent many days in the kitchen with her mom and grandmothers which developed in her a love for cooking for others. Stephanie has been married to her wonderful husband, Matthew, since 2004 and they have 3 children, all of whom love to help out in the kitchen. She is living her dream of owning a log house in the country and she now cooks many of her meals on a wood cook stove just like her grandma used to. Stephanie loves to be creative in the kitchen and had her own cake decorating business, Sweet Designs by Stephanie, for 3 years. She also worked as a chiropractic assistant for several years, has her Medical Transcription Certificate and has taught a variety of classes at Algonquin College in Pembroke and out of her home. She currently hosts a monthly Healthy Lifestyle Club in Pembroke where she demonstrates how to cook healthy meals and educates others on the benefits of a total vegetarian lifestyle. In the future, she would like to expand these meetings into other towns. In addition, Stephanie is studying to be a medical missionary and hopes to do some missions work with her family teaching others in underdeveloped countries about Biblical health and wellness.

A Note of Thanks:

A special thank you goes out to my two Grandmothers – Esther Gorr and Gert Folber – for their devotion to cooking, baking and preserving and handing down these seemingly "lost arts". I appreciate all they did and they both truly inspired me to be who I am today.

I am also thankful to my mom – Liane Folber – for tirelessly teaching me how to cook, bake, can, and preserve. She has also answered many a phone call asking her to remind me how long to cook something, how many pounds of pressure something requires for canning, or just to listen when I tell her about a new recipe or project I'm working on.

Thank you to my wonderful husband, Matthew, who never tires of eating things that sometimes don't turn out and who is always willing to try something new. He has taught me that it's ok to be flexible and creative when I'm cooking and has encouraged me in many other ways as well.

And most importantly, I am thankful to the Lord for putting these people in my life to help me along the way and for guiding my steps into His paths of truth. *1 John 2:1-17*

The Inspiration for this Cookbook:

Before my family and I made the transition to a total vegetarian lifestyle, I had been dealing with a gluten and dairy allergy for several years. I quite often found myself searching the internet and cookbooks for new recipes to try and would always come away discouraged. Most of the gluten free recipes I was finding contained dairy products of one kind or another and I was beginning to get very frustrated with this. One day, however, I was searching online for recipes and it occurred to me that I should search for gluten free *vegan* recipes because they would naturally contain no dairy products. Once I came to this conclusion, my once-mundane task of endless searching for recipes seemed to be over.....for a while. I did find, however, another roadblock once we adopted a plant-based diet: there is a very limited selection of plant-based AND gluten free recipes that actually taste good and aren't loaded with unhealthy fillers like refined sugars, unnecessary oils and fats, unique and hard-to-find ingredients or pre-made alternative "convenience" foods (like vegan cream cheese, vegan mayonnaise, cheese-substitutes, etc.) that are both expensive and hard to find if you don't have access to the large variety of health food stores and specialty markets that are common in larger cities.

Since deciding to venture out and make a cookbook, I've had several people tell me that they are vegetarian or vegan AND gluten free. In addition, some of those people are endlessly searching for good recipes to no avail. I see the need for this type of cookbook and I hope and pray that it will be a blessing to those who have been searching for a collection of recipes designed to meet their dietary and financial needs.

About this cookbook:

When you hear the name *"Cooking For Life"*, it can bring to mind several different ideas. This name stood out to me because it encompasses 3 different thoughts, all of which, I believe, are important to good health.

1. _Cooking for a lifetime_ – A lifetime of cooking is inevitable, whether we're cooking for ourselves or whether someone else is doing the cooking for us. What we choose to cook, eat and drink is a choice we all have to make every day. Ultimately, these choices will be a determining factor in our health and quality of life.

2. _Cooking for our lives' sake_ – The quality of life we experience is largely based on what we put into our mouths. We are seeing the many advantages of moving away from the typical North American Diet (which is largely animal-protein based) and adopting a plant-based lifestyle. It is this plant-based diet that the Lord Himself implemented at Creation in the Garden of Eden (Genesis 1:29) and He knew that we would thrive on this simple way of eating. Some of the advantages of a total plant-based lifestyle include reversing diabetes, cancer, heart disease, depression and high blood pressure. In many cases, there's also the added benefit of weight loss. Gluten-free living is also gaining exposure as more and more people are discovering they have either a sensitivity or an allergy to gluten. According to www.gluten.net, gluten intolerance is the number one undiagnosed disorder in the US. Also, for every one person diagnosed with a gluten intolerance, 80 people go undiagnosed. Gluten is found in wheat, rye, barley, spelt, kamut and triticale. It's also found in oats that are cross-contaminated with other gluten-containing grains

(wheat/barley/rye-free oats are now more readily available, however), so it's not an easy task to cook gluten free. So much of what we are accustomed to eating and cooking with contain these ingredients that can be toxic to many. Anyone who is living with a food allergy can attest to the fact that they are indeed Cooking for Life.

3. _Cooking for spiritual life_ – The Bible says "know ye not that your body is the temple of the Holy Ghost which is in you, which ye have of God, and ye are not your own?" 1 Corinthians 6:19 KJV. If at all possible, whenever we discover the healthiest way to live, we have a responsibility to follow this as good stewards of the body that we have been given. "Whether therefore ye eat, or drink, or whatsoever ye do, do all to the glory of God." 1 Corinthians 10:31 KJV. The best way for us to share Christ with others is not in being sick and unhealthy. While a sick person still has the power to minister to others, one of the most powerful witnesses one can have is a strong and healthy mind and body that is able to discern and teach spiritual things. "The health of the body is to be regarded as essential to growth in grace and the acquirement of an even temper. If the stomach is not properly cared for, the formation of an upright moral character will be hindered. The brain and nerves are in sympathy with the stomach. Erroneous eating and drinking results in erroneous thinking and acting." E.G. White, Review and Herald Mar. 3, 1910

How we cook and eat for our lives is something that we all must consider. _"Cooking for Life – A Total Vegetarian, Wheat Free and Gluten Free Cooking Experience"_ is a cookbook that is designed to help those who want to live a healthier lifestyle without giving up delicious food. It is perfect for those who have adopted a plant-based lifestyle, are wheat and/or gluten free, both, or neither! I've tried to include recipes that are made with ingredients that are easy to find and fairly inexpensive. All of the recipes are free from meat, fish, shellfish, eggs, dairy, casein, wheat, rye, barley, spelt, kamut, millet and triticale. I have included wheat-free oats in some of my recipes but I have noted them near the top of each recipe. Many people who are unable to tolerate gluten are able to use wheat-free oats without a problem. And most recipes are free of refined sugars and are low in fat, making it easier to enjoy a little extra from time to time. I hope you enjoy these recipes as much as my family and I do!

Please note: "Gluten Free" in Canada means that the food does not contain wheat, spelt, kamut, rye, barley, oats or triticale or any parts thereof. I have, however, included wheat free oats in some of my recipes. I have not included any other known gluten-containing grains in my recipes. Although oats that are certified free from wheat, rye and barley are available and a great option for many suffering with gluten and/or wheat intolerances and allergies, there are some individuals that are still sensitive to uncontaminated oats. I have made a note at the top of any recipe that contains oats so you are able to choose if that recipe is right for your particular dietary needs. Please check with your health care practitioner or natural health specialist before consuming wheat/barley/rye free oats if you are concerned that you may react.

A few words about living without wheat and gluten:

I have been living a gluten-free lifestyle for over 10 years and was on a wheat-free diet for 5 years before that. Gluten free cooking is something that I do every single day and although it's a challenge, it's still possible to make healthy food that is delicious too. I have experienced cooking flops and failures along the way and am very fortunate that I have a husband that didn't mind eating them anyway! As daunting as it might seem when one is first advised to refrain from eating gluten-containing foods, it's not as overwhelming if you have accurate and helpful information and some good, tried and true recipes. I can understand firsthand how helpful and appreciated a good gluten free cookbook is and it's also important that the recipes be practical and not full of hard-to-find ingredients or complicated instructions. I hope this cookbook will be a "go-to" book for many people who are dealing with a gluten intolerance or allergy as well as a resource book for those who might not be gluten-free but are wanting to cook for others who are. I have included some of my favorite health-related websites, businesses and restaurants in the "Resources" section of the book and some gluten free "tips" throughout various recipes that will hopefully make you and your loved ones' gluten-free journey less worrisome and more delicious!

How a Plant-Based Lifestyle has changed our lives:

Our family began our plant-based journey in 2010 shortly after I had our third child. We were presented with the idea that eating meat and animal-based foods was the source of many diseases and that God's original diet that was given in the Garden of Eden (fruits, grains, nuts and seeds) was how God had intended for us to be nourished. While growing up, I had many health concerns but in most cases, I stumped the physicians and explored alternative means of getting well. I sought chiropractic and nutritional therapy and although these things resulted in better health for me, it became expensive and inconvenient for me to continue on in that course. It did, however, encourage me to continue on with my passion for learning more natural means of curing illnesses and diseases.

My husband was diagnosed with severe sleep apnea less than a month before we got married in 2004. Typically, at that time, sleep apnea had been reserved for overweight and underactive individuals. My husband didn't fit into either of these categories so for him to be diagnosed with this condition was baffling. Over the next few years, both of us became unhealthy and less active than before. My husband's weight went up to 270 pounds at his heaviest and was having occasional heart palpitations. We were chronically overtired and stressed and our children were suffering from some "common childhood illnesses" – asthma, croup, eczema, chronic ear infections and joint pain.

After doing some research on the benefits of a plant-based lifestyle, we decided that it was a good and healthy choice. Over time, we adopted other healthful living practices and in the three years that we have been eating this way, my husband has lost over 75 pounds. He has also been given a clean bill of health regarding his sleep apnea (which the doctors can't explain) and chronic health issues for both him and me have disappeared. Our children no longer suffer from the illnesses they were once plagued with and none of them have had a prescription or taken any medication for over two years. We can say firsthand that a plant-based diet has changed our lives and I hope and pray that our experience will shed some light on the subject for anyone who may be searching out options for their health.

Please note – before adopting a plant-based diet, please consult with your health care practitioner. We have had much success with a plant-based diet but our experience is in no way meant to determine your own individual outcome. There were several factors that determined our success and although changing our diet was extremely beneficial, our improved health was not only based on eliminating animal products, but also adopting other health principles. If you have any health concerns, please consult with your health care practitioner before undergoing any major dietary changes.

A Note on the importance of B12:

Vitamin B12 is an important vitamin, playing a key role in brain and nerve function as well as in the formation of blood. Unfortunately, it is not found in most plant foods. In order for vegetarians and vegans to get enough of this important vitamin, they need to be certain to include vitamin B12-fortified foods or a B12/folic acid supplement into your daily routine. There aren't very many gluten free options for obtaining B12 in food sources, so a B12/Folic Acid supplement might be the best option to ensure an adequate amount of B12 is being consumed. B12 should always be taken with folic acid, however. If our bodies are deficient in Folic Acid, taking B12 alone will drive our Folic Acid stores down even further. Similarly, if we are low in B12 and take a Folic Acid supplement, it will cause our B12 levels to go down if we are deficient. Having either a B12 or Folic Acid deficiency can cause serious health problems if not properly diagnosed and/or treated.

Seaweed and products like tempeh are generally not reliable sources of vitamin B12. Often, nutritional yeast is suggested to supply B12 but unless B12 is specifically added and noted on the label, nutritional yeast is not a reliable source of B12 either. Vitamin B12 is found in many multivitamins and in vegetarian supplements. Be sure to read the label to ensure the product is gluten free and not enclosed in a gelatin capsule.

Life lessons from the kitchen:

How often are you baking or cooking and you have *just* the right amount of an ingredient you need for your recipe and not a bit more? Like when you need 3 cups of flour and you have exactly 3 cups in the bottom of your bag and you don't have another bag. That happens to me all the time. Something like that happened to me a few months ago where I needed 9 Tablespoons of ground flax seeds for a recipe. I wasn't able to grind anymore because my grinder (which is also my soy milk maker) was in use making soy milk and would be unavailable to use for about 30 minutes. I needed the flax to make a recipe right then so having the right amount was important. So as I was scooping out the ground flax from my jar, I was watching and hoping that I had enough but it wasn't looking good. But as I got to the 9th tablespoon, I had exactly that much and not an ounce more. I got to thinking how often that happens to me in the kitchen and thought that maybe the Lord was trying to tell me something. I thought some more on it and came to the conclusion that God works the same way in our lives. He gives us exactly what we need, when we need it. When it looks like there's not enough of something – money, resources, time, help, etc. – whatever it is, He is willing to supply our needs if we ask Him. *"Be careful (anxious) for nothing; but in everything by prayer and supplication with thanksgiving let your requests be made known unto God." Philippians 4:6 "But my God shall supply all your needs according to His riches in glory by Christ Jesus". Philippians 4:19*

Everything we need, He will supply.....even in the kitchen.

Breakfasts

Favorite Fruit Smoothie

This smoothie is very versatile and a great way to incorporate extra fruit into your breakfast! Add fresh or frozen fruit of your choice and change up the juice and you can have a different and delicious smoothie every day. If you're feeling extra adventurous, try adding some fresh leafy greens and you've got a nutrient-packed start to your day.

Makes 4 servings

- 4-5 cups frozen fruit or a mixture of fresh and frozen – some of our favorites are strawberries, bananas, mangos, peaches, pears, pineapple and applesauce
- 1 ½ - 2 cups 100% fruit juice or water (or enough to blend to desired consistency) – cherry, blueberry, orange or mixed berry juice are delicious
- Greens (optional) – kale, swiss chard, spinach or romaine lettuce

1. Place all ingredients in a blender and blend until smooth. Pour into glasses.

Stephanie's Suggestions
- A high-powered blender or smoothie-maker is beneficial but not necessary. If you don't have a high-powered blender such as a Vitamix or a Bosch Mixer, you may have to add some extra liquid to make blending easier.
- Read the labels carefully when looking for juice. Make sure it's 100% fruit juice with no added sugars or artificial sweeteners. Some of the juices that are available also contain unexpected ingredients such as green tea extract or clam juice so be sure to check the ingredients before you buy!

Creamy Orange Smoothie

This delicious smoothie reminds me of the orange cream popsicles that I enjoyed as a child. Have one of these in the morning and it feels like you're having dessert for breakfast!

Makes 2-3 servings

- 2 ½ cups orange juice
- 1 large banana, fresh or frozen
- 5 oz. silken tofu
- Ice cubes (optional – only needed if not using a frozen banana)

1. Place all ingredients into a blender and blend until smooth. Serve. Doubles really well.

Stephanie's Suggestions
- Silken tofu is very soft and is best used in smoothies and desserts. It has a milder flavor than other types of tofu which makes it a great choice for adding creaminess to recipes without the added cholesterol and fat of dairy-based creams.
- Tofu is a great way to add high-quality, low fat plant-based complete protein to your diet as well as the added benefits of fibre and b-vitamins.

Carob Mint Green Smoothie

I came up with this smoothie recipe with hopes of increasing the greens in our family's diet in a way that the kids would love. This delicious smoothie reminds me of mint chocolate ice cream! The kids devour it and they have no idea how good it is for them!

Makes 2 large or 3 medium servings

- 3-4 cups chilled almond or soy milk, unsweetened vanilla or regular
- 2 frozen bananas, cut in chunks
- 6 Tbsp carob powder
- ¼ tsp mint extract (or to taste) *OR* a small handful of fresh mint leaves
- 3 cups packed fresh spinach

1. Add all ingredients into a blender in order given.
2. Blend well and pour into glasses.

Stephanie's Suggestions

- Instead of composting your overripe bananas, why not slice them up and freeze them for a quick and delicious addition to smoothies? The riper they are, the sweeter they will taste. And frozen bananas are the secret to a super creamy smoothie!
- Spinach and all leafy greens are super healthy and are best eaten raw. There is more calcium in spinach than in red or white meat. Also the calcium in spinach is in a form that is very easily digested. It's also very high in iron. We eat less of green leafy vegetables than all other vegetables so this delicious smoothie is a great way to get them in.
- Iron is best absorbed when paired with vitamin C so enjoy this smoothie with a fresh orange or grapefruit and a bowl of gluten free granola with soy or almond milk topped with fresh berries and you will have a delicious breakfast that will nourish your body and make you feel great!

Almond Milk

Finding something delicious to replace cow's milk with can be challenging. Almond milk is a great choice whether you're first making the transition to dairy-free or even if you've been following a plant-based diet for a while. Its flavor is mild and nutty and can be used in most recipes to replace milk cup for cup.

Makes 4 cups

- 2/3 cup almonds, soaked for 4-6 hours
- 5 cups water
- ½-1 tsp vanilla, optional
- stevia or other sweetener to taste, optional

1. Place nuts and water in a blender. Blend on high speed until smooth. It's ok if your blender isn't powerful enough to pulverize everything.
2. Strain milk into a jug or glass canning jar using a fine mesh sieve or cheesecloth.
3. Add optional vanilla and stevia and stir. Store in refrigerator. Keeps for up to 2 weeks.

Stephanie's Suggestions
- If you're using the almond milk for savory things like mashed potatoes or biscuits, omit the vanilla.
- Soaking the almonds isn't necessary but soaking does makes them easier to blend, easier to digest and releases their full nutritional value.

Quick and Easy Fruit Salad

This fruit salad is so simple that my 7 and 4-year-old boys offer to make it for breakfast quite often. It's a basic recipe designed to give you the freedom to change it however you want with whatever fruit you might have in the fridge, freezer or pantry.

Serves 5

- 1 large banana, sliced
- 2 cups fresh or frozen strawberries
- 1 cup canned or fresh pears
- ½ cup canned or fresh peaches
- 1 apple, diced
- 1 orange, peeled and cut into chunks
- 1 cup fresh or frozen blueberries or mixed berries

1. The night before, take out any frozen berries and place in a bowl to thaw.
2. In the morning, add remaining ingredients, stir and serve.

Stephanie's Suggestions

- Try using this fruit salad as a topper for pancakes with a drizzle of pure maple syrup.

Orange Tapioca Fruit Salad

Traditional tapioca is made with eggs, milk and lots of sugar. Although this is not quite the same as the tapioca pudding that most people are used to, it's a great breakfast or dessert option. And as a bonus, tapioca is naturally gluten free!

Makes 6-8 medium-large servings

- 2 cups orange juice
- 2 cups sliced bananas
- 1/3 cup tapioca, uncooked
- 14 oz or 19 oz can pineapple tidbits, reserving juice
- ½ cup shredded coconut, sweetened or unsweetened
- 2 cups green seedless grapes, halved
- 2 small cans mandarin orange sections or 1 large jar, preferably packed in juice, drained

1. Cook tapioca in orange juice over medium heat until clear, approximately 10 minutes once it comes to a boil. Stir often as it will stick fairly easily.
2. Remove from heat, stir in coconut and chill.
3. Once chilled, stir to break up tapioca. Add bananas, pineapple, grapes and mandarin oranges. Add enough pineapple juice to make pudding the desired consistency (usually ¾ of the can).

Stephanie's Suggestions
- Tapioca is a starch that is extracted from the cassava plant. Interestingly, it's gluten free, virtually protein free and contains practically no vitamins!

Breakfast Power Bars

Chewy, fudgy and oh so good!

Makes 24 1x2 squares or 12 large bars

- 2 cups walnuts
- 2 cups dates
- ½ cup unsweetened coconut
- ¾ cup carob powder
- 1 Tbsp melted coconut oil (melt by placing over hot water)
- 1 Tbsp pure vanilla extract
- ¼ tsp coconut extract
- ½ cup liquid honey

1. Place walnuts in food processor that has been fitted with the "S" blade. Grind walnuts until very fine.
2. While the food processor is running, add dates. Once all the dates are mixed, turn off the machine and add the carob powder, coconut oil, vanilla and coconut extract. Pulse to mix.
3. Turn on processor and slowly add honey. The mixture should be sticky enough to hold together when pressed but not so sticky that it sticks to your hands. Add more honey if necessary to get the mixture to stick together.
4. Press into 8" square pan and refrigerate until completely firm, at least 1 hour. Keep chilled. Freezes well.

Julie's Seedy Bars

I was given this recipe by our prenatal class teacher, Julie Keon, at the end of our 8-week set of classes. They are an excellent source of fibre, iron and protein as well as a host of other vitamins and minerals – perfect for new mothers or anyone wanting a delicious breakfast option.

Contains Oats

Makes 1 pan

- 1 cup wheat free steel cut oats
- 1/3 cup dried cranberries, blueberries or currants
- ½ cup pumpkin seeds
- ½ cup sunflower seeds
- ½ cup raisins
- ¼ cup prunes, chopped
- ¼ cup psyllium husk
- ¼ cup ground flax seeds
- ½ tsp cardamom
- ½ tsp coriander
- 1 cup peanut butter or other nut butter
- ½ cup liquid honey or pure maple syrup

1. Combine first ten ingredients and then stir in nut butter and honey or maple syrup. Mix well.
2. Press into rectangular glass baking dish that has been sprayed with cooking spray or rubbed with oil. A pan that's slightly smaller than a 9x13 is best or you can use 2 pie plates.
3. Bake at 325*F for approximately 20 minutes. Cool completely before cutting.

Light and Fluffy Pancakes

Is it possible that a name like "light and fluffy" can really be describing something gluten free? Well it's true! Even if you're not gluten free, you'll enjoy these too.

Makes 8-10 4" pancakes

- 1 ¼ cups non-dairy milk such as soy, almond, hemp or flax milk
- 1 tsp lemon juice
- ½ cup unsweetened applesauce
- 1-2 tsp pure vanilla extract
- Oil for pan (coconut oil is best)
- ½ cup brown rice flour
- ½ cup buckwheat flour
- ¾ cup tapioca flour
- 2 Tbsp pure maple syrup
- ¾ tsp xanthan gum
- 1 tsp baking powder
- ¾ tsp baking soda

1. Preheat skillet or griddle. Brush with a light layer of oil or cooking spray.
2. Pour non-dairy milk into a 4 cup measuring cup. Add lemon juice to non-dairy milk and set aside for a few minutes to sour.
3. Meanwhile, in a medium mixing bowl, stir together dry ingredients.
4. Once the milk has soured, add in remaining wet ingredients and stir to combine.
5. Add wet ingredients to dry and whisk together well. The mixture will get a little thick because the buckwheat flour tends to absorb a lot of liquid. If you prefer a thinner pancake batter, add a little water or non-dairy milk until the batter reaches the desired consistency.

6. Using a small ladle or spoon, scoop batter onto preheated griddle. Cook until edges look set and there are little bubbles on the surface of the pancake. Flip and cook for another couple minutes until the bottom is golden.

Stephanie's Suggestions

- Try adding fresh fruit to the pancake batter for a different twist! Diced apples, peaches, nectarines or blueberries are great additions and will also stretch the batter a little further.
- Using flavored applesauce will give a nice change of taste.
- For a different topping, we often will use peanut butter and jam or peanut butter topped with applesauce that has been mixed with a couple spoonfuls of jam and then warmed.
- For a decadent breakfast treat, top these pancakes with fresh or canned peaches, non-dairy vegan whipped topping and pure maple syrup. Delicious!

Some of the largest and strongest animals in the world – the elephant, giraffe, rhinoceros, hippopotamus, gorilla, oxen, cow, buffalo, and moose – are all vegetarian.

"If you want to be strong like a strong animal, you must not eat the animal, but you must eat the same things that the strong animal eats. If the animal is strong because he eats the proper natural diet, let us eat the proper diet also, – the diet God gave us."
Dr. J. H. Kellogg

Berry Crisp

Delicious warm right out of the oven! If you're serving this for dessert instead of breakfast, try topping it with Banana Coconut Ice Cream. Then again, the Banana Coconut Ice Cream recipe is healthy enough that you could have it for breakfast too! Yum!

Contains Oats

Makes 6-8 servings

- 1/3 cup honey
- ¼ cup water or melted coconut oil
- 2 cups wheat free oats, quick or large flake
- ½ cup brown rice flour
- ½ cup chopped pecans
- 2 Tbsp cornstarch or 3 Tbsp brown rice flour
- 1-283 mL can frozen apple juice concentrate, thawed
- 1 tsp lemon juice
- 3 cups sliced, fresh strawberries
- 2 cups fresh blueberries
- 1 cup fresh blackberries

1. Preheat oven to 350*F.
2. In a small bowl, combine honey and water (or coconut oil) until blended. Stir in the oats, flour and pecans until blended. Set aside for topping.
3. In a glass measuring cup or small bowl, combine the cornstarch and ¼ cup of the apple juice concentrate until smooth. A whisk works really well.
4. In a saucepan, combine the lemon juice and remaining apple juice concentrate. Gradually whisk in the cornstarch mixture. Bring to a

boil; cook and stir until thickened, about 3-5 minutes. Remove from heat, add berries and stir.
5. Place berry mixture in a 9x13 glass baking dish that has been sprayed. Sprinkle with oat mixture. Make sure the topping is level and even.
6. Bake, uncovered, in preheated oven for 25-30 minutes or until bubbly and top is golden brown

Stephanie's Suggestions

- Fresh berries are ideal for this recipe but don't be afraid to use frozen too! Just keep in mind that you will have a lot more juice to deal with so your crisp might come out a little moister than if you were using fresh berries. It tastes great either way!
- Change up the fruit for a different flavor. Try combining raspberries, blueberries, and peaches or get creative and make your own version! You can also add ¼ tsp each of ground cardamom and coriander to the apple juice mixture.
- Please note – if you're used to having sweet foods, you may find this and other refined sugar-free recipes not as sweet as you may be used to. It takes time for our palettes to change so keep trying! In the meantime, you can always add a little bit of sugar to help in the transition from sugar-laden to sugar-free

"For people with diabetes, a total vegetarian diet was all it took for blood glucose levels to decrease significantly."
Dr. David Jenkins and Dr. Neal Barnard

4-Step Granola

It's difficult to get enough fibre when you're eating wheat and gluten free. Incorporating quality wheat-free oats into your diet is a great way to increase your fibre intake. ½ cup of wheat-free oats provides 15% of the daily recommend amount of fibre (4g) as well as 25% of the recommended amount of iron.

Contains Oats

Makes approximately 20 cups

- 12 cups wheat free rolled oats– large flake OR quick
- 2 cups unsweetened shredded coconut
- 1-2 cups pecans, walnuts or whole almonds
- 1 283mL can frozen apple juice concentrate
- ½ cup honey
- ¼ cup pure vanilla extract
- 2 cups Raisins, dried strawberries, dried currants or other dried fruit of your choice
- 1 cup EACH pumpkin or sunflower seeds AND 1 cup sliced almonds, optional
- Ground flax seeds

1. Preheat oven to 250*F. In a large roasting pan sprayed with cooking spray or 2 9x13 sprayed baking dishes, combine oats, coconut and nuts (except sliced almonds). Toss lightly to mix.
2. In a small saucepan, combine apple juice concentrate, honey and vanilla. Warm over medium heat until honey is melted and liquid ingredients are combined. Pour warmed apple juice mixture over dry ingredients in roasting pan and mix thoroughly.

3. Bake, uncovered, in preheated oven for 3 hours. Stir at least once every hour. When baking time is done, turn oven off and leave granola in oven overnight.

4. In the morning, add raisins or other dried fruit, ground flax seeds, pumpkin or sunflower seeds and sliced almonds. If you choose to add the ground flax seeds, the granola will need to be kept in the refrigerator as ground flax seeds will become rancid if they are not refrigerated. Otherwise, store in an airtight container in a cool, dark place such as a cupboard or pantry.

Maple Apple Muffins

I love baking with apples! They are so versatile and can be used in everything from pies to crisps to cookies – and in this case, muffins. For a softer baked apple, try using varieties such as Empire, Spartan, Cortland or McIntosh.   If you prefer an apple that retains its shape and texture, stick with firmer apples like Royal Gala or Granny Smith.

Makes 12 muffins

- 1 cup soy, rice or almond milk mixed with 1 tsp lemon juice (if you don't have soy milk on hand, you can also use 2 Tbsp soy milk powder mixed with 1 cup water)
- 1 ½ Tbsp ground flax seed mixed into ¼ cup warm water
- ½ cup applesauce
- ½ cup pure maple syrup or ¼ cup syrup and ¼ cup brown sugar
- 2 cups diced apples (about 3 medium)
- 1 cup brown rice flour
- ½ cup sorghum flour
- 2 Tbsp tapioca starch
- 2 Tbsp potato flour (NOT starch)
- 1 tsp xanthan gum
- 1 tsp baking soda
- 1/3-1/2 tsp EACH cardamom and coriander
- 1 tsp salt
- Sucanat or maple sugar for sprinkling, optional

1. Mix soy milk with lemon juice and set aside. Likewise, mix ground flax with warm water and set aside for 10 minutes. Meanwhile, preheat oven to 350*F and peel, core and dice apples.
2. In a large mixing bowl, combine applesauce, flax seed mixture and maple syrup. Stir well.

3. Add apples and soy milk mixture. Stir in dry ingredients (except Sucanat) and mix well.
4. Spoon into sprayed muffin tins. Sprinkle with ¼ tsp Sucanat or maple sugar.
5. Bake in preheated oven for 22-25 minutes or until toothpick inserted in muffin comes out clean.
6. Let cool in muffin tin for 10-15 minutes before removing and placing on a wire rack to cool completely.

"Beloved, I wish above all things that thou mayest prosper and be in health, even as thy soul prospereth." 3 John 2

Orange Oatmeal Muffins

This is an old family favorite that I've adapted to be healthier. The combination of orange juice, oatmeal and raisins makes a delightful breakfast muffin.

Contains Oats

Makes 12-14 muffins

- 1 cup wheat free rolled oats (quick, not large flake)
- ½ cup orange juice
- ½ cup boiling water
- 1/3 cup virgin coconut oil, melted
- 1/3 cup sucanat, turbinado sugar or brown sugar
- 3 Tbsp ground flax seeds mixed with ½ cup warm water
- 1 cup raisins
- 1 cup gluten free flour blend **OR**:
- *1/3 cup sorghum flour*
- *1/3 cup brown rice flour*
- *1/3 cup combination of quinoa and chickpea flour*
- 1 tsp xanthan gum
- 1 tsp baking powder
- 1 tsp baking soda
- 1 tsp salt
- 1 tsp vanilla

1. In a 1-cup measuring cup, mix together ground flax seeds and ½ cup warm water. Set aside.
2. In a small bowl, soak oats in orange juice and boiling water for 15 minutes.
3. Preheat oven to 350*F.

4. In large bowl, combine coconut oil and sugar. Add flax and oat mixtures and stir well.
5. Stir in raisins and remaining ingredients. Fill greased muffin cups and bake in preheated oven for 20 minutes or until toothpick inserted in the middle of a muffin comes out clean.

Banana Oatmeal Breakfast Muffins

Super simple and quick to whip up is a great way to describe these muffins. The hardest part will be waiting for them to cool!

Contains Oats

Makes 6 muffins

- 2 medium bananas, mashed
- ½ cup large flake wheat free rolled oats
- ½ tsp cardamom
- ½ tsp coriander
- ½ tsp baking soda
- ¼ cup pure maple syrup
- 1 tsp pure vanilla extract
- ¼-1/3 cup raisins

1. Preheat oven to 375*F
2. Combine all ingredients in a medium bowl and mix well. Let rest for 5 minutes.
3. Spoon mixture into paper-lined muffin tins and fill to ¾ full.
4. Bake for 10 minutes. Reduce heat to 350*F and continue baking for an additional 8-10 minutes.

Apple Crisp

It might seem strange to include a recipe for Apple Crisp in the "Breakfast" section of a cookbook but because there are no refined sugars, good quality whole grains, nuts and lots of fruit, we enjoy this crisp for breakfast quite often.

Contains Oats

Makes 1 9x13 pan

- 1 can apple juice concentrate
- 1 Tbsp lemon juice
- 1 tsp cinnamon substitute (1/2 tsp each cardamom and coriander)
- ¼ cup rice flour mixed with ½ cup water
- 8 cups peeled, cored and sliced apples – Macintosh or Empire apples work great
- 1/3 cup honey
- ¼ cup water or melted coconut oil
- 2 cups wheat free oats, quick or large flake
- ½ cup brown rice flour
- ½ cup chopped walnuts

1. Preheat oven to 350*F. Combine apple juice concentrate, lemon juice and cinnamon substitute in a large pot. Combine first amount of rice flour and water together and add to apple juice mixture. Cook over medium high heat until thick, stirring constantly.
2. Remove from heat and add apples. Stir to combine and pour in a sprayed 9x13 glass baking dish.
3. In a small bowl, combine honey and water (or coconut oil) until blended. Stir in the oats, ½ cup rice flour and walnuts until blended. Sprinkle evenly over apples.
4. Bake in preheated oven for 35-45 minutes or until topping is golden brown.

Scrambled Tofu

Replace scrambled eggs with this delicious entrée! Packed with flavor and protein, it will help you "get cracking" in the morning without ever having to crack an egg!

Makes 5 servings

- 1 420g pkg firm tofu (not silken or extra firm), drained and rinsed
- 1 medium onion, chopped
- 2 cloves garlic, crushed
- 1 green or red bell pepper, chopped
- Vegetables of your choice – some good options are sliced mushrooms, cabbage, zucchini, or grated carrots
- 3-4 cups baby spinach
- 1 Tbsp chicken-style seasoning *(See Miscellaneous)*
- 2 Tbsp nutritional yeast
- ½ tsp turmeric

1. Place onions, garlic and red or green pepper in a skillet. Sautee in a small amount of water until onion and pepper is softened, about 5 minutes. Add vegetables of your choice and continue cooking until softened.
2. Crumble tofu into frying pan with your hands. Add chicken-style seasoning, nutritional yeast and turmeric. Stir well to distribute seasonings.
3. Add baby spinach. The spinach will shrink down significantly with cooking. Cover frying pan for a few minutes to "steam" the spinach and then remove the lid to continue cooking tofu for another 5-10 minutes or until most of the moisture is gone. Stir often while cooking.

Southwestern Breakfast Wraps

These might be called "Breakfast Wraps" but they can be enjoyed at any meal. A variety of beans can be used so feel free to change it up!

Makes 10-12 wraps

- 1 recipe Scrambled Tofu *(See Breakfasts)*
- 2 cups pinto beans, cooked and seasoned to taste with chili powder substitute *(See Miscellaneous)*
- garlic powder, onion powder and salt
- 2 cups salsa *(See Sauces and Dips)*
- Lettuce
- Sliced Black Olives
- Green peppers (optional)
- 12 Gluten free wraps or large romaine lettuce leaves

1. Prepare Scrambled Tofu according to directions.
2. Place a wrap on a plate and spread a layer of scrambled tofu in a line down the centre of the wrap. Top with beans, lettuce, olives, peppers and salsa.

Stephanie's Suggestions
- Beans and legumes are naturally low in fat and high in fibre. See "Miscellaneous" section for a comprehensive chart on cooking dried beans and legumes.
- Because beans are not a complete protein, it's a good idea to either pair them with "complementary" foods such as grains or flours or make sure that somewhere throughout the day, you have a grain as part of another meal. This will fill in the amino acids that the beans are lacking. Some good combinations include beans and tortillas, beans and rice and beans and pasta.

Potato Patties

These potato patties go well with scrambled tofu and a side of sliced tomato. The key to a crispy outside is the chickpea flour – no other flour will do quite the same job!

Makes 12 patties

- 4 cups mashed potatoes or leftover stamppot *(See Sides)*
- 1 large onion, chopped finely
- 3/4-1 cup chickpea flour
- Oil for frying
- Salt to taste

1. Combine cooled mashed potatoes or stamppot and onion in a bowl.
2. Preheat griddle or frying pan to medium high. Brush lightly with oil.
3. Form potato mixture into 1/3 cup patties.
4. Place ½ of the chickpea flour on a dinner plate or glass pie plate. Coat both sides of each patty with flour and place on hot griddle. Fry until golden, approximately 5-8 minutes. Flip patty and continue cooking the other side until golden.
5. Add chickpea flour to the plate as necessary. You don't want to add it all at once as the flour will become too moist from the potatoes and not coat the patties as well.
6. Season cooked patties with salt to taste and serve hot.

~For optimal digestion, incorporate fruits into one meal and have vegetables at another~

Notes:

Soups, Salads and Sandwich Fixings

Honey Molasses Sandwich Bread

This is a great loaf of bread! Why buy expensive gluten free bread in the store when you can make it for so much less? In order to get the best results, a heavy duty stand mixer is a definite asset. This loaf freezes well, doubles well and makes a great toasted tomato sandwich.

Makes 1 loaf

- 1 ¾ cups brown rice flour
- ¼ cup tapioca flour
- ¼ cup potato starch
- ½ cup sorghum flour
- 1 Tbsp xanthan gum
- 1 Tbsp instant yeast
- ½ tsp salt
- 4 ½ Tbsp ground flax seeds mixed with ¾ cup warm water
- 1 cup warm water (additional amount)
- 1 tsp lemon juice
- 2 Tbsp vegetable oil
- 2 Tbsp honey
- 2 Tbsp fancy or unsulfured blackstrap molasses (blackstrap will yield a stronger flavour)

1. In a 1-cup measuring cup, combine ground flax seeds and ¾ cup warm water. Let sit for 10 minutes.
2. In a large bowl, combine flours, xanthan gum, salt and yeast. Set aside.
3. Using the bowl of a heavy duty mixer fitted with the paddle attachment, combine 1 cup warm water, lemon juice, oil, honey, molasses, and flax mixture. Mix on low speed until well combined.
4. Slowly add dry ingredients to wet. With the mixer on medium speed, beat dough for 3-4 minutes.

5. Scrape dough into lightly greased loaf pan. Press down dough with wet hand or wet spatula to make the top level. Let rise, uncovered, in a warm spot for 45-60 minutes or until dough has reached the top of the pan. I like to turn my oven on to the "keep warm" setting and set it to 145*F.

6. When dough is finished rising, set oven to 400*F. Bake at 400*F for 15 minutes. Lower oven to 350*F and continue baking an additional 20-25 minutes.   Cool for at least 15 minutes before trying to take the loaf out of the pan.

Stephanie's Suggestions

- While blackstrap molasses is the healthier choice, being rich in iron, calcium, folate and magnesium, fancy molasses will yield a milder-flavored bread. Blackstrap molasses will give a more robust flavor to your loaf.
- This recipe doubles really well but you have to make sure your mixer has a bowl large enough to accommodate that much dough. A 5.5 quart bowl or larger is an ideal size.
- If you don't have a heavy-duty mixer, try mixing the dough vigorously with a wooden spoon or spatula. This will result in a more dense loaf but still tasty nonetheless. A traditional hand-held mixer is not recommended as the dough is too thick and sticky and the beaters on the mixer are generally not long enough to handle it.

Onion Bread

Not your typical bread recipe! This is a very unconventional way to make bread – no flour and baked flat on a cookie sheet. If you have a dehydrator, you can even make this "raw" which preserves the nutrients better than cooking does.

Makes 2-3 cookie sheets

- 1 cup ground flax seeds
- 1 cup warm water
- 3 medium onions, thinly sliced
- 2 large carrots, grated
- 1 tsp salt
- 3 Tbsp olive oil

1. Combine flax seeds and water, stir and let sit for 10 minutes.
2. Meanwhile, in a food processor, slice the onion into thin pieces. Additionally, grate the carrots in the food processor. Mix onions and carrots together with remaining ingredients.
3. Add flax combination to onions and mix well.
4. Line dehydrator trays with parchment paper. Alternatively, line 2-3 cookie sheets with parchment paper. Spread mixture thinly on pans – as thin as the thickest piece of onion.
5. If using a dehydrator, dry at 105*F for a couple of hours. When top is no longer sticky and slightly dry, flip over and continue drying. Dry until firm but not crispy.
6. If using your oven, bake at lowest temperature possible (usually a "keep warm" setting will work well for this) and flip when top is slightly dry. Continue baking until firm but not crispy, usually another couple of hours.
7. Cut into large "bread slice-sized" squares using kitchen shears or a pizza cutter.

Stephanie's Suggestions

- Pair this onion bread with avocado, sliced tomato and a stack of alfalfa or clover sprouts for a delicious, healthy sandwich – which is naturally gluten free!
- Onions contain a mild antibiotic that fights infections, soothes burns, tames bee stings and relieves the itch of athletes foot

"And Jesus said unto them, I am the bread of life: he that cometh to me shall never hunger; and he that believeth on me shall never thirst." John 6:35

Chickpea "Tuna" Salad

Chickpeas are known throughout the world by many different names including garbanzo beans, ceci (pronounced she-she) beans, chana, sanagalu, Gonzo Beans and Bengal gram. Whichever name you know them by, they are delicious in this sandwich spread which is reminiscent of a tuna salad sandwich – without the cholesterol or risk of mercury consumption.

Makes approx. 2 cups

- 1 ½ cups cooked chickpeas (or 1-15 oz can)
- 1/4-1/2 cup creamy garlic spread *(See Sauces and Dips)*
- 1/3 cup minced celery
- 1 Tbsp zucchini relish *(See Soups, Salads and Sandwich Fixings)*
- ½ Tbsp nutritional yeast
- 1-2 green onions, chopped
- 1 tbsp gluten free soy sauce or tamari sauce
- Vegetable salt to taste

1. In a medium bowl, mash the chick peas with a potato masher. Mix in remaining ingredients and serve on gluten free bread or toast, gluten free wraps or wrap it up in large romaine lettuce leaves. Great topped with lettuce or spinach and accompanied by Lemony Dill Pickles on the side!

Eggless "Egg" Salad

This is pretty close to the real thing! Toast up a couple pieces of Honey Molasses Sandwich Bread, add a leaf or two of lettuce or spinach and you have a great sandwich that is filling and nutritious.

Makes 4 cups

- 1-420g package of firm tofu, drained and rinsed
- ½ cup chopped celery
- 1 onion, minced
- ¼ cup Zucchini Relish, *(See Soups, Salads and Sandwich Fixings)*
- 1 Tbsp chicken-style seasoning, *(See Miscellaneous)*
- 1 tsp turmeric
- ½ tsp garlic powder
- ¾ cup Creamy Garlic Spread, *(See Sauces and Dips)*

1. Crumble tofu into a medium bowl. Add remaining ingredients and mix well. Store in an airtight container in the fridge.

Stephanie's Suggestions
- Although this tastes best the same day it is made, it still is great as leftovers the next day and keeps well for 4-5 days.
- It's normal for separation to occur. Simply stir mixture before using.

Caesar Salad and Dressing

Traditional Caesar Salad is a double offender where a plant-based gluten free diet is concerned. Caesar dressing quite often contains wheat as well as milk products, eggs and anchovies. Add in the croutons and real bacon bits and you have a recipe for a food disaster! But I have good news for you– you CAN enjoy Caesar salad again with this delicious recipe that is naturally gluten, dairy, egg and meat free!

Makes 2/3 cup

Dressing:
- 4-5 Tbsp freshly squeezed lemon juice
- 2 Tbsp cold pressed extra virgin olive oil
- ½ cup water
- ½ cup cashews or sunflower seeds, or half and half
- ¼ cup Parmesan Cheeze Please, *(See Miscellaneous)*
- 2 cloves garlic
- ½ tsp salt

Salad:
- 1 head romaine lettuce
- Garlic powder
- Onion powder
- Additional Parmesan Cheeze Please
- Gluten Free meatless bacon bits, optional

1. To make the dressing, place lemon juice, olive oil and water in a blender and blend until well mixed.
2. Add cashews or sunflower seeds, Parmesan Cheeze Please, garlic and salt. Blend until smooth.

3. For salad, wash, chop and spin romaine lettuce and place in a large salad bowl. Sprinkle with garlic powder, onion powder and additional Parmesan Cheeze Please to taste, usually ¼ -1/2 tsp.
4. Add meatless bacon bits and top with dressing. Only use as much dressing as necessary. Toss well to mix. The salad will shrink down once the dressing is on so if it looks like a lot of lettuce, it will get smaller!
5. Top with gluten free, vegan croutons if available.

Stephanie's Suggestions

- Variation: For a delicious entrée, replace the romaine lettuce with hot, cooked gluten free pasta. Adjust seasonings to taste and serve!
- Pair this salad with gluten free spaghetti or lasagna and gluten free garlic toast for a great meal.
- You can use either cashews or sunflower seeds in this recipe. Cashews will yield a creamier and more flavorful dressing but cashews are more expensive and contain more fat than sunflower seeds.

Garden Fresh Salad

Salads are a great and versatile way to get a variety of fresh vegetables into our diets. There are so many ways that salads can be prepared – the choices are endless! I've included a few of my favorite ways to spruce up a traditional garden salad so you can take it beyond iceberg lettuce and tomatoes!

Makes 5 large servings

- 1 head romaine lettuce or a mixture of romaine, spinach and leaf lettuces or other greens
- 1 tomato, diced
- ½ English cucumber, sliced
- 10-12 baby carrots, sliced
- 1 bell pepper, any color
- 1 sweet potato, baked, peeled and cubed (slightly warm or cool)
- 1-2 baked potatoes, cooked and cubed (slightly warm or cool)
- 6-8 grilled asparagus spears, optional
- 1 avocado, peeled, pit removed and cubed
- ¼-1/2 cup pepitas (shelled pumpkin seeds)
- 1 recipe roasted chickpeas *(See Sides)*
- Cold, cooked seasoned quinoa (to cook and season quinoa, take 1 cup dried quinoa and add 2 cups water and 1 Tbsp chicken-style seasoning. Bring to a boil and cook, covered, for 20 minutes)
- ½-3/4 cup radish, alfalfa or clover sprouts or other sprouts of your choice
- Gluten free, vegan dressing of your choice

1. Wash and cut lettuces, spinach or greens. Place in a large salad bowl.
2. Prepare remaining vegetables and add to lettuce. Toss and serve with dressing of your choice.

Stephanie's Suggestions

- As a healthy and convenient alternative to a head of lettuce, try any of the prewashed and prepackaged greens that are now available at many grocery stores (some options are swiss chard, tat soi, kale, mustard greens and dandelion greens mixes). They boost the nutritional value while adding a great variety of textures and flavors to a salad.
- Dandelions might seem like weeds, but the flowers and leaves are a good source of vitamins A and C, iron, calcium and potassium. One cup of dandelion greens provides 7,000-13,000 I.U. of vitamin A. So when the dandelions are taking over your lawn, instead of fighting against them, embrace them and add a handful to your salad!
- Pumpkin seeds are a nice addition to salads. They are loaded with fiber, vitamins, minerals, and many health promoting antioxidants. They are delicious when added to granola or trail mix too!

"Getting well is EASY. It is getting sick that takes years of constant, dedicated hard work." – Dr. Shulze

Perfect Potato Salad

Potato Salad is perfect for any picnic – and this one is no exception! Usually potato salad is reserved for summer fare but serving it at other times of the year is not unheard of – it's one of my husband's favorites so we find any reason we can to have it!

Makes 12 large servings

- 3 lbs potatoes, peeled and cut into chunks
- 2 stalks celery, diced
- 1 medium onion, minced
- ½ - 2/3 cup Lemony Dill Pickles, chopped *(see Soups, Salads and Sandwich Fixings)*
- ½ tsp garlic powder
- 1/3 tsp turmeric
- 2 Tbsp Chicken-style seasoning *(See Miscellaneous)*
- 3 Tbsp Nutritional yeast
- 1 tsp onion powder
- 2 ½ cups Creamy Garlic Spread *(See Sauces and Dips)*

1. Several hours before serving, prepare potatoes. Peel and cut potatoes, place in a large pot, cover with water, bring to a boil and simmer, covered, until tender – about 15-17 minutes.
2. Drain potatoes, mash and transfer to a large serving bowl. Refrigerate for a few hours or until cool.
3. Meanwhile, chop celery, onions and pickles. Place in bowl with cooled potatoes.
4. Add seasonings and Creamy Garlic Spread. Mix well and chill until ready to serve. If preparing in advance, you may need to add a bit more Creamy Garlic Spread before serving depending on how creamy you like your potato salad.

Lemony Dill Pickles

Dried dill is used in these pickles so you can make them any time of the year – all you need is a glass jar, a few ingredients and the patience to wait 24 hours until they're ready!

Makes 1-1L jar

- ½ cup lemon juice, fresh or bottled
- 2 Tbsp salt
- 2-3 cloves garlic, sliced
- 1 tsp dried dill
- 1 large English cucumber
- 1L glass jar with lid (a large canning jar works perfectly)

1. Fill glass jar with lemon juice, salt, garlic and dill.
2. Slice cucumbers into rounds. Fill jar with cucumber slices. Fill jar with water and cover with lid. Shake briefly to combine all ingredients.
3. Put in refrigerator and let sit for 24 hours. These will keep in the fridge for at least 2 weeks. They never last in our house that long though!

Stephanie's Suggestions

- We use these pickles as a great alternative to the traditional vinegar-brined dill pickles. Vinegar increases our body's acidity which makes us more prone to disease and illness. Vinegar also decreases the blood clotting factor in our blood. Family favorites like these pickles can still be enjoyed with the addition of lemon juice instead of vinegar.

Zucchini Relish

Relish and pickles are typically made with vinegar, sugar and irritating spices such as mustard, peppercorns, cloves and other spices. Not only are these things unnecessary, they are also very irritating to the stomach and the digestive system as a whole. Try this honey-sweetened relish and you may never go back!

Makes approximately 20-25 250mL jars

- 1 ½ cups water
- 6 cups chopped onion
- 3 cups EACH chopped red pepper and chopped cauliflower
- 3 Tbsp salt
- 1 ½ cups honey
- 1 ½ tsp turmeric
- 1 ½ cups lemon juice
- 1 ½ tsp celery seed
- ½ tsp coriander
- ½ tsp rosemary
- 18 cups chopped zucchini
- ¾ cup arrowroot starch mixed with 1 ½ cups water

1. In a large pot, sauté onions and red pepper in a little water. Add cauliflower and seasonings and mix well.
2. Add honey and zucchini. Bring to a boil and cook over medium heat. When vegetables are tender yet firm, add flour and water. Continue cooking until thick.
3. Remove from heat and ladle into hot, sterilized 250 mL glass jars. Process for 15 minutes in a boiling water bath to ensure against spoilage.

Stephanie's Suggestions

- This recipe makes a LOT so feel free to reduce by half or even ¾.
- Because it is sweetened with honey and not sugar, this relish only lasts a few days in the fridge once it's opened. It's best to use smaller jars rather than larger ones.

"Tart words make no friends; a spoonful of honey will catch more flies than a gallon of vinegar" Benjamin Franklin

French Lentil Salad

We love this salad! It's so versatile – serve it hot, cold or at room temperature. It can also be used as a side or main dish. It travels well for potlucks or lunch at work and requires only a few ingredients.

Makes 10-12 servings

- 12 oz French lentils (smaller than green lentils)
- 3 garlic cloves, slightly smashed with the flat side of a large knife
- 1 clove garlic, minced (additional amount)
- 1 tsp salt
- ½ cup cold-pressed extra virgin olive oil
- Zest and juice from 1 lemon (approximately 3 Tbsp juice)
- 2 medium or 1 large carrot, peeled and finely diced

1. Place lentils and smashed garlic into a medium pot. Add enough water to cover by 2 inches, cover pot and bring to a boil over high heat. Reduce heat to medium-low and simmer for 10 minutes. Add salt, stir and simmer for 10 more minutes.
2. Turn off heat and let lentils sit for 15 minutes. Drain. At this point, you can either discard the garlic or you can mash it and stir it in to the lentils.
3. Pour drained lentils into a medium bowl and let cool. Add remaining ingredients and season with salt. If serving cold, chill for several hours.

Stephanie's Suggestions
- French lentils are usually found in health food store rather than in a grocery store. They are smaller than green lentils and require less water when cooking. They also retain their shape and firmness better than green lentils making them ideal for this salad.

Sesame Peanut Dressing & Dipping Sauce

This Asian-inspired dressing goes great not only on a garden-fresh salad, but also makes a wonderful dipping sauce for Rice Paper Rolls *(see Side Dishes)*.

- ¼ cup unsalted peanuts
- 1/3 cup nutritional yeast flakes
- 1/3 cup lemon juice
- ½ cup water
- ½ cup toasted sesame oil
- ½ cup cold pressed, extra virgin olive oil
- 2 cloves fresh garlic
- 1 tsp onion powder
- 1 tsp marjoram
- 1 tsp salt
- 2 ½ tbsp honey

1. Measure all ingredients into a blender and blend until smooth. Pour into glass canning jar or other glass container and store in refrigerator. This dressing keeps for approximately 2 weeks in the fridge.

Dill Dressing

This creamy dressing is a nice addition to any garden salad. This recipe can be easily cut in half if you're not planning on using it up quickly.

Makes approximately 3 cups

- ½ cup raw, unsalted sunflower seeds
- ½ cup tahini (sesame seed paste)
- 2 tsp onion powder
- 1 ½ tsp salt
- 1 ¼ cups water
- ½ cup lemon juice, fresh if possible but bottled works well too
- 2-3 cloves garlic
- 1 tsp dill weed
- 1 Tbsp dried parsley flakes

1. Place all ingredients into a blender and blend until smooth.

Stephanie's Suggestions
- If your blender is not very powerful, try soaking the sunflower seeds for a couple hours first. This will soften them up and make blending them much easier.

Toasted Tomato Sandwich Supreme

Nothing says summer like garden fresh tomatoes! This "grown-up" version of the classic sandwich is sure to please – but who's to say that kids won't love it too?

Makes 2 sandwiches

- 4 slices Honey Molasses Sandwich Bread *(See Soups, Salads and Sandwich Fixings)*
- Creamy garlic spread *(See Sauces and Dips)* or Caesar salad dressing *(See Soups, Salads and Sandwich Fixings)*
- 1 medium tomato, sliced
- English cucumber, sliced
- ½ avocado
- Lettuce or spinach
- Alfalfa or clover sprouts
- Sea salt to taste

1. Toast bread to desired doneness. Spread Creamy Garlic Spread or Caesar dressing on each slice. Top with tomato, cucumber, avocado, lettuce or spinach and sprouts. Sprinkle on a little sea salt to taste and enjoy!

~Knowledge is knowing a tomato is a fruit.
Wisdom is not putting it in a fruit salad ~

Split Pea Soup

This soup tastes just as delicious without the traditional hambone – and without all the extra fat and calories.

Makes 12 cups

- 2 ¼ cups dried split peas
- 8 cups water
- 2 onions, diced
- 2 tsp salt
- 1 pinch dried marjoram
- 3 stalks celery, chopped
- 3 carrots, chopped
- 2 medium potatoes, diced in ½ inch pieces
- 2 cups diced turnip, optional
- 1 bay leaf

1. In a large pot, combine all ingredients. Cover and bring to a boil. Reduce heat and simmer for 1 ½ hours, stirring occasionally.
2. Doubles or triples well and freezes beautifully.

Corn Chowder

When we switched to a total vegetarian diet, I was blessed to come across a set of three wonderful cookbooks – LifeStyle Matters "Guilt Free Gourmet". This recipe, from Volume 3, was one of the first recipes I made and it quickly became a family favorite.

Makes 12 1-Cup servings

- 1 cup cashews
- 4 cups frozen corn or fresh off the cob
- 1 onion, chopped, sautéed in water
- 6 cups potatoes, peeled, cubed and cooked
- 3 Tbsp chicken-style seasoning
- ¼ cup nutritional yeast flakes
- 1 tsp basil
- ¼ tsp savory or sage
- 2 tsp onion powder

1. Cook onions and potatoes together in a little water until tender. Blend 2 cups of the onion/potato mixture with the cashews and ½ cup of the corn.
2. Add enough water to blend smoothly to a thick, creamy chowder. Leave the remainder of the corn and potatoes chunky.
3. Add more water to mixture to reach the desired consistency. Add all other ingredients and warm through.

Stephanie's Suggestions
- A special thanks to LifeStyle Matters for allowing me to include some of their wonderful recipes in this cookbook. For more information on their program or to get additional recipes, please visit www.lifestylematters.com

Potato Spinach Soup

This simple yet delicious soup is sure to get two thumbs up – even from the kids!

Makes 10-12 cups

- 1 large or 2 medium onions, chopped
- 4-5 cloves garlic, minced
- 5 large potatoes, peeled and cubed
- 8 cups water
- 1 bag (approximately 8-10 cups loosely packed) fresh spinach, chopped
- 3 Tbsp chicken-style seasoning *(see Miscellaneous)*

1. In a large pot, sauté onions and garlic in a small amount of water. When softened, add potatoes, water and seasonings. Cook until potatoes are tender, approximately 10-12 minutes.
2. Add spinach and cook a few minutes more until spinach has wilted down.
3. Blend soup in small batches in blender and pour into another pot or serving dish.

"The brain is the organ and instrument of the mind, and controls the whole body. In order for the other parts of the system to be healthy, the brain must be healthy. And in order for the brain to be healthy, the blood must be pure. If by correct habits of eating and drinking the blood is kept pure, the brain will be properly nourished."
E.G. White, Medical Ministry

Notes:

Sauces & Dips

Creamy Garlic Spread

This is a delicious spread that can be used in a variety of ways. It can replace mayonnaise in a dip, dressing or salad and can also be used as a sandwich spread.

Makes 2 cups

- ½ cup sunflower seeds
- ½ cup water
- 1-17.5 oz package of silken tofu
- 3 ½ Tbsp lemon juice
- 1 tsp salt
- 1 tsp garlic powder
- 1 ½ tsp onion powder

1. Place all ingredients in a blender and blend until smooth. Will thicken as it chills.

Stephanie's Suggestions
- Soaking the sunflower seeds in water for a few hours beforehand will help them blend up more smoothly.
- This will keep for approximately 1 week in the refrigerator.

Barbecue Sauce

Barbecue sauce is a great way to add pizzazz to a meal. This is a great recipe because there are no refined sugars and irritating vinegar like the commercial varieties have. It also works as a replacement for ketchup and is perfect topping for my Lentil Loaf.

Makes 3 ½ cups

- 3 cups tomato puree (1-5.5 oz/156mL can tomato paste mixed with enough water to equal 3 cups)
- 5 tbsp blackstrap or fancy molasses
- ½ cup honey
- 2 tsp onion powder
- 1 Tbsp garlic powder
- ½ Tbsp parsley flakes
- 3 tbsp gluten free soy sauce
- 2 tbsp lemon juice

1. Place all ingredients in a saucepan. Bring to a boil, reduce heat and simmer for 10 minutes

Stephanie's Suggestions

- Tomato sauce is generally made from less-than-acceptable tomatoes and quite often is loaded with salt and sugar to give it a better flavor. Tomato paste, on the other hand, is made with top quality tomatoes. As a general rule of thumb, you can make your own tomato sauce by combining 1 5.5oz can with 2 cups water.

Salsa

If you're like me and you like to do lots of canning and preserving, this is a must-have recipe for the abundance of summer tomatoes. A jar of homemade salsa also makes a great gift or housewarming present or pair it with corn chips for a quick and simple appetizer tray when unexpected guests drop by.

Makes 2 ½ quarts

- 4 ½ pounds ripe tomatoes, heirloom if possible
- 1 large Spanish onion or 2 medium cooking onions
- 1 green pepper, chopped
- 1 red pepper, chopped
- 2-3 jalapenos, carefully seeded and chopped (wear gloves!)
- 1-5.5 oz can tomato paste
- ¾ cup lemon juice
- Stevia to taste or ¼ cup brown sugar or Sucanat
- 1 Tbsp coarse salt
- 2 tsp paprika
- ½ tsp garlic powder
- 5x1 pint glass Mason jars
- 5 lids and rings for jars

1. Scald tomatoes by placing them in a large bowl or your sink and covering them with boiling water. Let sit for a few minutes until skins start to peel off. Carefully drain or dump water. Slip peels off, remove stems and cores and chop coarsely. Place in a large pot.
2. Combine remaining ingredients with tomatoes. Bring to a boil, stirring occasionally. Reduce heat to medium-low and simmer for 1-1 ½ hours or until liquid has been reduced and it reaches the desired consistency.

3. In the meantime, wash glass jars and sterilize in a 250*F oven for 10 minutes. Turn oven off and keep warm until ready to use. This should be done just before you're ready to fill the jars.
4. When salsa has thickened up enough, fill hot sterilized jars using a canning funnel. It is important that you fill the jars while the salsa is very hot or the lids won't seal properly.
5. Wipe rim of jar clean and top with lid and ring. Let sit, undisturbed, on the counter until cooled. Make sure that each lid is sucked down. If any lids fail to seal properly, store in refrigerator and use within 7-10 days.

Stephanie's Suggestions

- Because this salsa is made with lemon juice and not vinegar, it only keeps for approximately 7-10 days in the refrigerator once opened.
- For a different flavor and texture, add some cooked and cooled black beans, corn and cilantro just before serving.
- It's important to sterilize all canning equipment to ensure against spoilage. Sterilize metal utensils by boiling in water for several minutes and heat clean glass jars in a 250*F oven for 10 minutes.

Corn and Black Bean Salsa

If you want a quick and delicious appetizer that's perfect for summer, this is it! Garden fresh corn and ripe, fresh grape tomatoes make this a summertime favorite.

Makes 5-6 cups

- 1 can black beans, drained and rinsed
- 2 ears of fresh corn OR 1 small can corn niblets, drained
- 2 avocados, peeled, pit removed and diced
- 1 pint grape tomatoes, quartered
- 2-3 Tbsp lime or lemon juice
- Zest of 1 lime, optional
- 3-4 Tbsp chopped fresh cilantro
- Salt to taste
- Gluten free corn chips

1. Combine all ingredients in a medium bowl and gently mix. Serve with gluten free tortilla chips.

Stephanie's Suggestions
- Although this recipe calls for black beans, you can use other beans as well. A milder bean such as pinto or yellow eyed-beans would be a good alternative if you prefer something different than black beans.
- This salsa can easily be made into a cold salad instead of a salsa. Serve it alone or on a bed of greens for a delicious lunch option.

Gravy – Mmmm!

This gravy is delicious! Perfect on Neatballs, oven baked fries, mashed potatoes or whatever else you can think of!

Makes 5 ½ cups

- 1 cup unsalted cashews
- 1/3 cup cornstarch or ½ cup brown rice flour
- 4 cups water
- ¼ cup nutritional yeast flakes
- 2 tsp onion powder
- 2 Tbsp chicken-style seasoning
- ¼ cup sesame tahini

1. Blend all ingredients with 2 cups of the water in blender.
2. Pour into large saucepan. Pour remaining 2 cups water in blender and blend for a few seconds. This "cleans" the blender out and helps you not to waste any of the gravy. Pour water into pot with the rest of the gravy mixture.
3. Cook over medium heat, stirring constantly until thick. Remove from heat and serve.

Stephanie's Suggestions
- A special thank you to the LifeStyle Matters Team for allowing me to include this recipe. For more information or health tips, visit www.lifestylematters.com

Cheeze Sauce

This creamy cheese-style sauce is a wonderful topping to steamed vegetables, potatoes or our favorite – Haystacks! The jalapeno pepper is optional but it really does make this sauce extra nice.

Makes 3 cups

- ¼ cup unsalted cashews
- 2 ½ cups water
- ½ Tbsp lemon juice
- ½ red pepper, seeded and chopped coarsely
- ½ medium jalapeno pepper (approximately a 1 ½" piece), seeds removed, optional
- ¼-1/3 cup nutritional yeast flakes
- 1 tsp onion powder
- 1/3 tsp garlic powder
- ¼ cup brown rice flour
- 1 tsp salt or to taste

1. Blend all ingredients with 11/2 cups water in a blender until smooth.
2. Pour into saucepan and add remaining 1 cup water to the blender. Blend briefly for a few seconds. This "cleans" the blender out so as not to leave any of the delicious sauce behind!
3. Heat over medium heat, stirring often with a whisk until thick.
4. Serve hot. Keeps well for several days in refrigerator and reheats easily.

Stephanie's Suggestions
- Be sure to check the ingredients when buying cashews or other nuts. Choose nuts that are either raw or roasted and unsalted. Dry roasted nuts quite often contain wheat so make sure you read the ingredient list carefully.

- When cutting and removing seeds from jalapenos, it's best to wear gloves as the oils in the peppers can really irritate your skin. A melon baller works great at quickly extracting the seeds and veins from the pepper. Remember to remove your gloves carefully when done and do not touch your eyes, nose or mouth!

"To the health and happiness of the whole family nothing is more vital than skill and intelligence on the part of the cook. By ill-prepared, unwholesome food, the cook may hinder and even ruin both the adult's usefulness and the child's development. Or by providing food adapted to the needs of the body, and at the same time inviting and palatable, they can accomplish as much in the right as otherwise they accomplish in the wrong direction. So, in many ways, life's happiness is bound up with faithfulness in common duties."
E.G. White, Child Guidance

Hummus

We owe it to our Middle-Eastern friends for coining this delicious dish that is gaining popularity all over the world. It's naturally gluten free and makes a great dip, spread or sandwich addition.

Makes 3 cups

- 1 19-oz can chickpeas OR 2 cups soaked and cooked chickpeas
- ½ cup water plus additional water for blending
- ¼ cup lemon juice
- 1/3 cup tahini (sesame paste, NOT sesame butter)
- 2 tsp garlic powder
- 1 tsp onion powder
- 2-3 Tbsp chopped fresh dill or1 tsp dried dill weed
- 1 tsp sea salt
- ½-1 red pepper, raw or roasted, optional

1. Place all ingredients in a blender. Blend on medium or high speed, depending on your blender. Stop the blender to scrape down the sides and stir. Add enough extra water a tablespoon at a time, if necessary, to achieve a creamy consistency.
2. Store in an airtight container in the refrigerator.

Pizza Sauce

My mom taught me many things in the kitchen while I was growing up. She shared with me much advice, tips and recipes – including this one.

Makes 2 cups

- 1 onion, chopped in small pieces
- 1 5.5 oz can tomato paste
- ½ quart canned tomatoes, undrained
- 1 tsp dried basil
- 1 tsp dried oregano
- 1 tsp garlic powder
- 1 tsp onion salt OR a combination of 1 tsp onion powder and ½-3/4 tsp salt

1. Place onion in a frying pan or medium saucepan with a small amount of water. Sautee onion in water until soft. Add tomato paste, tomatoes, basil, oregano, garlic powder and onion salt.
2. Simmer for about ½ hour. This is enough for one pizza but it does make a fair amount. Any leftover sauce freezes well.

Honey Garlic Sauce

Serve this sauce on top of Neatballs or as a dip. And unlike most sweet and sour sauces, this one is free of refined sugars. It can be easily cut in half if you don't need such a large amount.

Makes approximately 4 ½ - 5 cups

- 2 Tbsp non-hydrogenated vegan margarine such as Earth Balance
- 16 cloves garlic, minced
- 2 red peppers, chopped (omit if using sauce as a dip)
- 28 ounce can of tomatoes
- 1 ½ cups honey
- ½ cup gluten free soy sauce
- 1 large can pineapple tidbits, drained or ½ fresh pineapple, peeled, cored and chopped into tidbit-sized pieces , optional (omit if using sauce as a dip)
- 1/3 cup cornstarch

1. Puree tomatoes in blender until smooth. Set aside.
2. Melt margarine over medium heat in a large saucepan. Add garlic and peppers and stir until soft. Add pureed tomatoes and honey. Heat until honey has melted and combines well.
3. Pour soy sauce into a glass 1-cup measure. Add cornstarch and stir well until smooth. Stir into tomato mixture. Bring to a boil, stirring often until thickened. Add pineapple and heat through.

Notes:

Side Dishes

Spicy Rice

The amount of heat in this recipe is entirely optional and up to you how hot you make it. For children, it's best to keep the heat very minimal but for adults, a little cayenne pepper or a whole red chili pepper is a nice addition.

Makes 6 servings

- 1 cup uncooked brown rice
- 2 cloves garlic, minced
- 2 cups cold water
- ½ onion, chopped
- 1 tbsp chicken-style seasoning
- ¼ cup salsa *(See Sauces and Dips)*
- 1 tomato, diced or ½ cup sundried tomatoes
- 1 red chili pepper, sliced lengthwise and seeds removed or ¼-1/2 tsp dried cayenne pepper
- Salt to taste

1. Add all ingredients to a large pot. Mix well. Bring to a boil. Turn heat to low, cover and cook the rice for 20 minutes if it's parboiled and 40 minutes if it's regular long or short grain rice. For best results, check individual package directions.
2. When the rice is cooked, it should be soft and fluffy. If all of the liquid is not absorbed, continue cooking with the lid off for a few minutes longer.
3. Adjust the seasonings to your tastes and serve hot as a side dish with Lentil Tacos, fajitas, enchiladas or burritos.

Stephanie's Suggestions

- Cayenne pepper is great in and out of the kitchen. While it's a nice way to add a bit of heat to any recipe, cayenne is also noted for being able to stop a heart attack in 30 seconds when mixed with water and consumed. In addition, if it is applied topically to a bleeding wound, it will stop the bleeding. Surprisingly, it does not burn when applied this way (as long as it's not put on any moist membranes such as nose, eyes, mouth, etc.). We keep a small container of it in our vehicles for "emergency use" and have found it to come in handy a number of times.

Baked Rice Pilaf

Baked rice is so delicious! It's pleasantly different in taste and texture than boiled or steamed rice. This is a nice dish where you can assemble all the dry ingredients in the morning and just before you're ready to cook it, add the liquid, pop it in the oven for an hour and forget about it until it's time to eat!

Makes 6 servings

- 1 stalk celery
- 1 small onion
- ½ green pepper
- 1 carrot
- 1 ½ cups uncooked brown rice (20 minute variety or parboiled)
- 2 ½ cups broth (1 Tbsp chicken style seasoning + 2 ½ cups boiling water)
- ½ tsp EACH salt and garlic powder
- 1 Tbsp non-hydrogenated vegan margarine, optional

1. Chop vegetables fairly small. Combine all ingredients in a sprayed 2 quart baking dish, stirring well. Cover and bake at 350*F for 1hour.

Stephanie's Suggestions
- This recipe doubles or even triples really well. It's a great dish for a crowd and is full of delicious vegetables. Even the kids love this one!
- If parboiled brown rice or 20 minute brown rice is unavailable, feel free to use regular brown rice but add ½ cup extra liquid and ½ hour to your baking time.

Grilled Vegetables

Barbecues seem to take the "backburner" when it comes to plant-based cooking. Gone are the days of meat patties, hotdogs, grilled chicken and fish. But never fear – your barbecue doesn't have to sit useless in the corner of your deck! These grilled vegetables give the barbecue a great comeback!

Serves 4-6

- 1 medium zucchini, cut into ½" rounds
- 1 large onion, cut in ½" chunks
- 1-2 green or red bell peppers, cut into 1" chunks
- 8 oz. mushrooms, halved
- Handful of cherry tomatoes, optional
- Olive oil
- Coarse salt to taste

1. Place cut vegetables in a large bowl. Toss with olive oil to coat and season with salt to taste.
2. Pour mixture into a grilling basket. Grill on medium heat for 20-30 minutes or until vegetables are tender, stirring occasionally.

Stephanie's Suggestions
- Try incorporating other seasonal vegetables such as asparagus spears or vary the types of onions, peppers and mushrooms for different flavors.

Nori Rolls

"Nori" is the Japanese name for a species of edible seaweed. It is dried and made into thin sheets that are traditionally used in making sushi. Seaweed is an excellent source of iodine, a mineral that is essential in proper thyroid function. These lovely little rolls are not only delicious but also full of nutrient-rich sprouts. Steamed brown rice can also be used in place of the sprouts.

Makes 3 rolls/18 pieces

- 1 package alfalfa sprouts or 3 cups homegrown alfalfa sprouts
- 1 EACH of Carrot and Avocado, sliced thin
- 3 Green onions
- ¼ of an English Cucumber, sliced thin
- 1 Red or green pepper, sliced thin
- Raw or toasted nori sheets
- Water for sealing nori sheets

2. Place a nori sheet, shiny side down, onto a cutting board. Spread a layer of sprouts to 1 ½ -2 inches below the top of the sheet.
3. Layer the vegetables along the bottom of the sheet. Working quickly, tightly roll nori sheet, starting at the end with the vegetables. To seal the nori sheet, dip your fingers into some water and moisten the top of the sheet where it was left empty. Lightly press moistened end together with roll to seal.
4. Slice rolls with a serrated knife. Repeat this process until you have the desired amount of rolls.
5. Serve with gluten free soy sauce, tamari sauce or dipping sauce of your choice.

Stephanie's Suggestions

- Typically, nori sheets are toasted but raw nori sheets are available in some health food stores. They are far superior in nutrition, vitamins and flavor compared to their toasted counterparts.
- See note on "Sprouting" in the "Miscellaneous" section for further information on sprouting your own seeds.

"The most indispensable ingredient of all good home cooking: love for those you are cooking for" Unknown

Rice Paper Rolls

Rice paper is a great way to make delicious salad rolls or "summer rolls". Packages of rice paper sheets are found in many grocery stores and are basically just round, crisp, translucent sheets made from rice starch and a few other ingredients. Usually they come in packages that have large quantities in them but they keep well for long periods of time so don't be afraid to grab a package and try these out!

Makes 12 rolls

- 12 rice paper sheets
- 3-4 cups alfalfa, clover or other sprouts of your choice
- Carrots, finely grated or sliced with a vegetable peeler
- Cucumber, thinly sliced
- Avocado, thinly sliced
- Peppers, thinly sliced
- Green onions, optional
- Lettuce or spinach
- Fresh Thai basil leaves, optional

1. Immerse 1 rice paper roll into a large bowl of warm water. Let soak for 5-8 seconds.
2. Remove from water and place on a dinner plate. Place sprouts and any other desired ingredients in the middle of the roll. Keep in mind that you don't want to fill it too full or the paper will break when rolling up. One piece of each vegetable is usually enough.
3. Roll the rice paper up: start with the right and left sides. Fold them in to the middle. Then, rolling tightly, start at the bottom and roll all the way up to the top. The moisture in the rice paper should be enough that it seals itself.

4. Place seam side down on plate or in a container. Cover with a damp paper towel and continue making the remainder of the rolls. Refrigerate, covered with damp paper towel, until ready to eat.
5. Serve with gluten free, vegan dipping sauce of your choice.

Stephanie's Suggestions
- Sesame Peanut Dressing & Dipping Sauce *(See Soups, Salads and Sandwich Fixings)* compliments these rolls perfectly.

"O taste and see that the LORD is good: blessed is the man that trusteth in him"
Psalm 34:8

Scalloped Potatoes and Onions

Potatoes and onions baked in a creamy sauce make for great comfort food without the addition of milk or cream.

Makes 6 servings

- 5 large potatoes, peeled and thinly sliced
- 1 large onion, thinly sliced or chopped (approximately 1 cup)
- 3 Tbsp non-hydrogenated vegan margarine such as Earth Balance
- ¼ cup brown rice flour
- 1 Tbsp chicken style seasoning *(See Miscellaneous)* mixed with 1 ¾ cups water
- 2 Tbsp Creamy Garlic Spread *(See Sauces and Dips)*
- ¾ tsp salt
- Paprika

1. Preheat oven to 325*F.
2. In a sprayed 2 ½ quart baking dish, layer potatoes and onions.
3. In a small saucepan, melt margarine and stir in flour until smooth (this makes a roux). Gradually add water mixed with seasoning, creamy garlic spread and salt. Cook and stir until thick.
4. Pour over potatoes and onions. Sprinkle with paprika, cover and bake in preheated oven for 1 ½ - 2 hours or until tender.

Stephanie's Suggestions
- When a recipe calls for an ingredient that makes a large quantity (like the Creamy Garlic Spread in this case) but only requires a small amount of it, I try to plan ahead with my meals and figure out other things that I could make to use up the leftovers. Plan to make Chick Pea Tuna Salad Sandwiches *(See "Soups, Salads, and Sandwich Fixings")* or Eggplant and Zucchini Bites *(See "Side Dishes")* so as not to waste the garlic spread. Waste not, want not!

Zucchini and Eggplant Bites

These are a fun a delicious appetizer or side dish. Gluten free, vegan breadcrumbs are more readily available now but if you want to make your own, simply grind a couple of slices of gluten free bread in a food processor.

- 1 medium zucchini, sliced into ½" rounds
- 1 Chinese eggplant, sliced into ½" rounds (Chinese eggplants are the long, skinny variety)
- ½ recipe Creamy Garlic spread *(See Sauces and Dips)*
- 3 cups gluten free bread crumbs mixed with 2 tsp Italian Seasoning, ½ tsp garlic powder and ½ tsp salt (or to taste)

1. Preheat oven to 325*F.
2. Pour bread crumbs into a pie plate and season.
3. Dip zucchini and eggplant rounds in garlic spread. Place in breadcrumbs and using a spoon, scoop breadcrumbs over top of vegetables, turning to coat.
4. Place on a sprayed cookie sheet and bake in preheated oven for 20-25 minutes or until golden brown and beginning to soften.

Stephanie's Suggestions
- This recipe is also great for onion rings. Just slice a couple of onions and separate them into rings. Prepare the recipe as above, baking for an additional 10-15 minutes or until golden brown.

Roasted Root Vegetables

The smell of these vegetables roasting is amazing! This is the perfect dish to warm you up on those cool fall days. It makes a wonderful meal when you pair it with Lentil Loaf, a tossed salad and Carob Pie for dessert.

Makes 6-8 servings

- 1 pound sweet potatoes
- 1 pound parsnips
- 1 pound turnips
- 1 pound carrots
- 2 Tbsp chopped fresh rosemary or 1 tsp dried, ground rosemary
- 3 tbsp chopped fresh sage or 2 tsp dried, rubbed sage (less if using ground sage)
- ¼-1/3 cup cold pressed extra virgin olive oil
- 1 head garlic, minced
- 1-2 tsp coarse sea or kosher salt or to taste

1. Preheat oven to 400*F. Peel and cut all vegetables into 1-inch pieces. Combine all ingredients in large roasting pan and toss to combine. Season with salt.
2. Roast for 1-1 ¼ hours, uncovered, stirring occasionally.

Stephanie's Suggestions
- Chunks of potatoes, onions, fennel bulbs or cabbage are also great additions to this mix.

Roasted Chickpeas

Chick peas are one of my favorite dried beans. They have a robust flavor and are very versatile. In addition, they are great sources of zinc, folate and protein and are very low in fat.

Makes 1 1/2 cups

- 2 cups cooked chickpeas or 1 19-oz can chickpeas, drained and rinsed
- ½-1 Tbsp cold pressed extra virgin olive oil
- ¼-1/2 tsp Cumin
- 1 Tbsp Garlic powder
- 1-2 tsp Onion powder
- ½-1 tsp Salt
- Pinch cayenne pepper (optional)
- 1 tsp Curry powder substitute (optional)

1. Preheat oven to 400*F.
2. Place chickpeas in a glass 8" or 9" square baking dish. Add seasonings to taste.
3. Drizzle with olive oil. Stir to coat.
4. Bake in preheated oven for 40-50 minutes, stirring occasionally, or until chickpeas have reached desired doneness. The longer you roast them, the crunchier they will get. Be careful that they don't burn, however.

Stephanie's Suggestions

- There are so many things you can do with these delicious little morsels! We especially love adding them to salads or eating them as a crunchy side dish.
- Double or triple the recipe and keep the leftovers in an airtight container in the refrigerator for a quick and easy addition of flavor, protein and fibre to a fresh garden salad.

Roasted Chickpea-Stuffed Acorn Squash

We really enjoy this dish in the fall when acorn squash are in abundance. They are the perfect size for individual portions and the kids love having their own little "squash cup" to eat right out of the shell.

Makes 4 servings

- 2 acorn squash
- 1 recipe Roasted Chickpeas, cooked and set aside *(See Sides)*
- Salt to taste

1. Preheat oven to 350*F.
2. Cut acorn squash in half horizontally so you have two similar sized pieces. Remove seeds and stem (if there is one).
3. Line two small or one large cookie sheet with parchment paper. Place squash cut side down on parchment.
4. Bake in preheated oven for 1 hour or until a fork can be easily inserted into the squash through the skin. You want the squash to be soft enough to scoop out but not so soft that the shell falls off. A lot of the beauty of this dish is in the presentation so you want to keep the skin firm enough to act as a bowl.
5. When baked, turn squash over and place on a serving platter. If the bottom of the squash has a point rather than a flat bottom, this will easily flatten down after it's been cooked.
6. Sprinkle squash with salt and fill the hole in the middle with ¼ cup of roasted chickpeas. If your chickpeas have cooled off too much, return to the oven for several minutes to warm them up again, being careful not to brown the tops of the squash too much.

Stephanie's Suggestions

- Another delicious way to stuff this squash is with a wild rice pilaf. Follow the same directions except using the pilaf instead of the chickpeas.

"And God said, Behold, I have given you every herb bearing seed, which is upon the face of all the earth, and every tree, in the which is the fruit of a tree yielding seed; to you it shall be for meat [food]." Genesis 1:29

Oven Roasted Jerusalem Artichokes

Jerusalem Artichokes are not a common vegetable and you'd be hard-pressed to find them in the grocery store. They are, however, very easy to grow. If you want to try growing these unique plants, you do want to make sure they stay separate from your other vegetables and flowers as they are known to take over very easily! They are a tall plant and have a beautiful yellow flower. Jerusalem Artichokes require very little work when growing but take a little more time when preparing. The results are rewarding though – delicious potato-flavored vegetables with a slightly nutty undertone.

Makes 4 servings

- 1 pound Jerusalem Artichokes, washed and cut in half or to uniform sizes
- 2-3 Tbsp olive oil
- Salt to taste

1. Preheat oven to 350*F.
2. Combine all ingredients in a glass 9x13 pan or roasting pan. Bake for 30-45 minutes, depending on the size of the artichokes. Bake until caramelized and tender.

Stamppot

Stamppot is translated as "mash pot" and is a traditional Dutch dish that is usually a combination of potatoes, vegetables or greens such as kale or swiss chard. Traditionally, sausage or bacon is cooked in with the potatoes but this vegan version is much healthier and still tastes great!

Serves 6

- 3-4 pounds potatoes, peeled and cut in large chunks
- 4 cups chopped fresh kale, swiss chard, spinach or other leafy greens or 1 pkg frozen spinach, thawed or left frozen
- Unflavored soy, almond or other non-dairy milk, optional
- Chicken style seasoning to taste
- Garlic powder to taste, optional
- Sea salt or vegetable salt to taste

1. Place potatoes and greens in a large pot. Fill with water and bring to a boil. Cover and cook for 12-15 minutes or until potatoes are tender.
2. Drain most of the water, leaving some to mash into the potatoes.
3. Mash potatoes and greens with the water. Using a hand-held electric mixer, whip potatoes until light and fluffy. Add additional non-dairy milk or water to desired consistency.
4. Season with optional chicken-style seasoning, garlic powder or salt.

Stephanie's Suggestions

- This side dish is a great way to get greens into your diet. Kale is our favorite to use because it is a powerhouse of nutrition, boasting generous amounts of fibre, calcium, vitamins, minerals and phytonutrients. Kids love this "healthy" version of mashed potatoes too!

Main Courses

Tex-Mex Shepherd's Pie

This is comfort food at its finest! Warm lentils and sauce, creamy mashed potatoes and sweet creamed corn make this dish a family favorite.

Makes 12 servings

- 4 lbs potatoes
- Soy, nut or rice milk, unflavored
- Non-hydrogenated vegan margarine (optional)
- Vegetable salt or regular salt, to taste
- 4 cups frozen mixed vegetables
- 1-2 green or red peppers
- 2 onions
- 2 Tbsp chili powder substitute
- 1 tsp cumin
- Pinch cayenne pepper
- 1 cup brown lentils
- 3 cups water mixed with 1 ½ Tbsp chicken-style seasoning *(See Miscellaneous)*
- 4 tbsp cornstarch mixed with a little water
- 2 small cans creamed corn

1. Heat a pot with a small amount of water. Add vegetables and seasonings. Cook for 5 minutes.
2. Add lentils and stock. Bring to a boil and simmer for 35-40 minutes or until lentils are tender. Add cornstarch mixed with a little water and salt to taste.
3. While the lentils are cooking, cook potatoes and mash together with non-dairy milk, optional margarine and salt.
4. Spread lentils in a large casserole dish. A deep dish casserole is best.

5. Top with mashed potatoes and creamed corn. Bake at 350*F for 30 minutes or until bubbly and heated through.

Stephanie's Suggestions

- This is the perfect dish to bring for a potluck! It also makes a quick and easy meal to bring to a new mother or a delicious and nourishing meal for a shut-in.
- This does make a lot so if you're making this for a smaller group, cut the recipe in half and prepare it in a small casserole dish.

"Whether therefore ye eat, or drink, or whatsoever ye do, do all to the glory of God." 1 Corinthians 10:31

Lentil Tacos

It's interesting to note that lentils are mentioned several times in the Bible, the first being the time when Jacob bought the birthright from Esau in exchange for a bowl of stewed lentils. Lentils were among the first foods that the Lord gave us and they haven't lost their appeal. They come in a variety of sizes and a rainbow of colors – red, green, brown, black, yellow and red-orange. They are also high in protein, fibre, vitamins and minerals making them a healthy and delicious source of nutrition.

Makes 6-8 servings

- 1 cup finely chopped onion
- 1 garlic clove, minced
- 1 cup dried brown lentils
- 1 tablespoon chili powder substitute *(See Miscellaneous)*
- 2 teaspoons ground cumin
- 1 teaspoon dried oregano
- 2 1/2 cups water mixed with 1 Tbsp chicken-style seasoning *(See Miscellaneous)*
- 12-16 gluten free hard corn taco shells or gluten free wraps

1. In a large saucepan, sauté the onion and garlic in a little water until tender. Add the lentils, chili powder substitute, cumin and oregano; cook and stir for 1 minute.
2. Add water mixed with chicken-style seasoning and bring to a boil. Reduce heat; cover and simmer for 25-30 minutes or until the lentils are tender. Uncover, mash lentils slightly with a potato masher and cook for 10 more minutes or until mixture has thickened. Serve on gluten free taco shells or gluten free wraps with your favorite toppings.

Stephanie's Suggestions

- We like topping these with simple ingredients such as shredded lettuce, vegan cheese or Cheeze Sauce *(See Sauces and Dips)* and salsa but feel free to be adventurous and add things like rice, avocado, tomatoes, sautéed mushrooms and peppers or anything else you like!
- This makes a great main dish – with or without the shells. Serve with salsa, rice, steamed vegetables and a tossed salad.

Lentil Loaf

Reminiscent of meatloaf, this delicious loaf is high in protein, fibre and iron without the cholesterol, fat and calories of Grandma's classic dish. Serve with mashed potatoes, steamed vegetables and Caesar Salad for a delicious, home-cooked meal that's sure to please.

Contains Oats

Makes 1 loaf

- 1 cup of brown lentils
- 2 1/2 cups of water with 1 Tbsp chicken-style seasoning *(See Miscellaneous)*
- 3 Tbsp of ground flax seed
- ½ cup of warm water
- 1 medium onion chopped
- 2 cloves of garlic minced
- 1 medium carrot grated
- 1 medium tomato, chopped
- ¾ cup chopped walnuts
- 1 tsp Italian Seasoning
- salt to taste
- ¾ cup of wheat free quick oats
- ½ cup of wheat free oat flour (you can make your own by processing wheat free oats in the food processor)
- Barbecue Sauce *(See Sauces and Dips)*

1. Mix ground flax and water together and let sit for 10 minutes.

2. Heat water mixed with chicken-style seasoning in a pot. When warm, add lentils and bring to a boil. Cover and simmer until water has been absorbed and lentils are cooked, approximately 40 minutes. Set aside to cool slightly.

3. Preheat oven to 350*F. Toast walnuts in the oven for 5-6 minutes. Watch carefully as they can burn rather quickly.

4. In a frying pan, sauté onion and garlic in a little water until onions are soft. Add carrot and tomato to heat through. Remove from heat and stir in walnuts.

5. Place ¾ of the cooked lentils in the food processor and process until smooth.

6. In a large bowl, combine all the ingredients. Stir well to ensure everything is well combined.

7. Spray a loaf pan with cooking spray and press the mixture firmly into the pan. Spoon barbecue sauce on top of loaf.

8. Bake in preheated oven for 40-45 minutes. Allow to cool for 10 minutes before slicing.

Stephanie's Suggestions

- Cook once, eat twice! Double this recipe to make two meals – and dirty the dishes only once! Throw one loaf into the freezer for a quick meal another time. Bake it ahead of time and then just warm it up before serving. Simple!

Fajitas

We love homemade Fajitas! Slice up some lettuce, grab a jar of homemade salsa and a bit of vegan cheese, add in a quality, gluten free wrap and you're all set!

Makes 10-12 fajitas

- 8-10 cups of a mixture of thinly sliced green and/or red peppers and onions
- 1-2 Tbsp olive oil
- 1 pkg extra firm tofu, sliced into ¼" sticks
- ½ cup water
- 4 Tbsp Fajita seasoning mix, or to taste *(See Miscellaneous)*
- Toppings such as lettuce, vegan cheese, cooked rice, vegan gluten free sour cream, and salsa
- Gluten free wraps

1. Heat olive oil in a large frying pan. Cook and brown tofu, stirring occasionally. Remove from pan and set aside.
2. Sautee onions and peppers in a little water in the same frying pan that the tofu was cooked in. Cook until soft, about 8-10 minutes.
3. Add tofu back to frying pan. Add ½ cup water and seasoning mix. Stir to combine. Cook until thickened, stirring often.
4. Serve hot on gluten free wraps with toppings of your choice. Also tastes great as a side dish with no wraps.

9-layer Dinner

A healthy spin on the classic "7-layer dinner".

Makes 8-10 servings

- Potatoes
- Onions
- Carrots
- Brown rice
- Cabbage
- Celery
- Peas
- 3 cups cooked pinto, kidney or other bean seasoned with 1 Tbsp garlic powder, 1 tsp onion powder and 1 tsp salt
- 1 quart Italian tomato sauce with 3 Tbsp brown rice flour and 2 tsp salt whisked in

1. Preheat oven to 350*F.
2. Layer each ingredient in a sprayed 5 quart casserole dish or small roasting pan.
3. Bake, covered, in preheated oven for 1 ½ hours, removing lid for the last 20 minutes. Watch that your beans don't dry out though!

Neatballs

No, that's not a typo! "Neatballs" are the vegetarian version of Meatballs. There are many different recipes out there for neatballs using a multitude of ingredients. A food processor helps to make this recipe quick and simple.

Contains Oats

Makes 20 1/8 cup Neatballs

- 2 cups raw, ground potatoes
- 1 Tbsp soy flour
- 1 onion, finely chopped
- 1 tsp rubbed sage
- 1 tsp basil
- 1 cup ground wheat free oats or gluten free bread crumbs
- 1 cup ground walnuts
- 1 ½ tsp salt
- 2 Tbsp Nutritional yeast flakes

1. Grind oats (if using), walnuts and potatoes in food processor or blender in that order (grinding the dry ingredients first eliminates the need to wash out the food processor between ingredients). Place in a large bowl.
2. Mix remaining ingredients into the bowl and stir well. Let mixture sit for 10 minutes.
3. Preheat oven to 350*F. Form mixture into balls and place on a sprayed cookie sheet or baking dish.
4. Bake 35-40 minutes at 350*F. Cover with spaghetti sauce, Honey Garlic Sauce (*See "Sauces and Dips"*) or vegan gravy *(See "Sauces and Dips")* and bake an additional 15 minutes, covered.

Stephanie's Suggestions
- Another great recipe from Lifestyle Matters! www.lifestylematters.com
- This recipe is a hit with meat-eaters and vegetarians alike!

Some of the most well-known men in history were vegetarians: Albert Einstein, Sir Isaac Newton, Thomas Edison, Leonardo da Vinci and Benjamin Franklin.

Barbecue Tofu

Tofu, simply put, is soy bean curd that has been packed into bricks. It's very versatile because it has the ability of taking on the flavor of whatever you pair it with. It can be savory or sweet, baked, scrambled, fried, boiled or blended and used in so many ways. This recipe does take a little bit of planning ahead but it is worth it! It is one of our favorite tofu recipes and both vegetarians and meat-eaters love it!

Makes 30-40 pieces

Drain and freeze 2-42oz packages of fresh, water-packed firm tofu at least overnight, then thaw

Basting mixture:
- 3 tbsp almond, peanut or soy nut butter
- ½ cup water
- 1 Tbsp paprika
- ½ tsp garlic powder
- ¼ cup nutritional yeast flakes
- 1 tsp salt

- 1 recipe Barbecue Sauce *(See Sauces and Dips)*

1. Combine all baste ingredients in a small bowl. Stir well to mix.
2. Preheat oven to 375*F. Slice the thawed tofu and cut each slice in half vertically so you have 2 squares per slice. Place them on a cookie sheet. With a small basting brush, spread the basting mixture generously on both sides of the tofu strips.
3. Bake in preheated oven for 25 minutes. Turn strips over and continue baking for an additional 25 minutes. Tofu should not be dark. You don't want to overbake them.
4. Place baked tofu in baking dish and pour Barbecue Sauce over them. Let sit for at least 3 hours. Bake at 375*F for 30 minutes. Serve over brown rice or alongside mashed potatoes and steamed vegetables for a delicious home-cooked meal.

Pizza

Pizza is definitely a personal thing when it comes to topping preferences. This is our favorite way to make a pizza – it requires a little bit of extra work but it's definitely worth it!

- 1 recipe Pizza Sauce *(See Sauces and Dips)*
- 1 large gluten free vegan pizza crust, unbaked
- Toppings such as mushrooms, broccoli, shredded vegan mozzarella-style cheese such as Daiya, olives, etc.
- 1 recipe of Caramelized Onions and Red peppers (see below)

1. Prepare pizza crust according to package directions. Top with sauce, caramelized onions and peppers and any other toppings of your choice.
2. Bake according to package directions.

Caramelized Onions and Red peppers

- 2 Tbsp cold pressed extra virgin olive oil
- 2 cups chopped onions – Vidalia are the best but any other onion will work as well
- 4 Tbsp chopped fresh parsley or 2 tsp dried
- 1 tsp dried basil
- Pinch of salt
- 1 sweet red and yellow pepper
- 3 cloves of garlic, minced

1. In a large skillet, olive oil over low heat. Cook onions slowly, stirring often, for about 45 minutes. Stir in parsley, basil and salt. Let cool slightly until you're able to handle it.
2. Meanwhile, place red and yellow peppers on baking sheet; broil, turning often, for about 15 minutes or until blackened all over. Let cool. Peel off charred skin, remove seeds, chop and add to onion mixture. Stir in garlic.

Crock Pot Beans

Crock pots are a great way to save you a lot of time in the kitchen. Prepare everything in the morning or the night before, assemble it in your crock pot and forget about it until supper. This recipe makes a lot so if you don't have a crock pot large enough or if you want a smaller amount, cut it in half. It tastes even better the next day so don't be afraid of leftovers!

Makes 20 servings

- 8 cups tomato puree (four 5.5 oz cans tomato paste mixed with enough water to make 8 cups)
- 2 tsp salt
- 2 medium onions, peeled and cut in half
- 2 additional medium onions, chopped
- 9 cloves garlic, minced
- ½ cup fancy molasses
- 14 cups cooked navy beans
- ¼ cup gluten free soy sauce
- ½-3/4 cup pure maple syrup
- 1 Tbsp dried rubbed sage (not ground), optional
- 1 tsp dried savory, optional

1. Put all ingredients into crock pot and stir well. Cook on low for 10-12 hours or on high for 5 hours.

Quiche

Traditionally, Quiche is made with a lot of eggs and milk. Try this plant-based version and you'll be surprised at how similar the results are – without the added cholesterol and fat.

Makes 1-9" Quiche

- 1 -420g package firm tofu, NOT silken or extra firm
- 1 pkg frozen spinach, chopped or whole leaf, thawed and excess water squeezed out
- 1/2 zucchini, diced
- ½ cup sliced green onions
- 1 medium green pepper, diced
- 1 cup fresh, sliced mushrooms
- 1/3 cup nutritional yeast flakes
- 2-3 Tbsp Chicken Style Seasoning *(See Miscellaneous)*
- 2-3 Tbsp cold pressed, extra virgin olive oil
- 1-2 cups vegan cheddar-style shredded cheese such as Daiya, optional
- 1-9" gluten free pie crust, NOT prebaked

1. Preheat oven to 350*F. Drain and rinse tofu and mash or crumble with your hands into a large bowl.
2. In a large frying pan, sauté zucchini, peppers, green onions and mushrooms in a little water until softened, about 5-7 minutes. Add vegetables and all remaining ingredients to tofu. Mix well and pack into unbaked pie shell(s).
3. Bake in preheated oven for 50-60 minutes or until firm with moisture gone. If the quiche is still slightly moist, put under the broiler for a few minutes but watch carefully so the crust doesn't burn!

Haystacks

Imagine healthy, delicious supreme-style nachos and you've got Haystacks!

Serves 4

- 3-4 cups cooked pinto, kidney or yellow-eyed beans, warmed
- Chili powder substitute *(see Miscellaneous)*, garlic powder, onion powder, salt – to taste
- Gluten free corn chips
- 8 cups shredded lettuce
- 1 ½ cups diced tomatoes
- 1 can sliced black olives
- 1 diced English cucumber
- 1-2 chopped red or green peppers
- 2 diced avocado
- 1 recipe Cheeze Sauce *(See Sauces and Dips)*

1. Season beans to desired taste with chili powder substitute, garlic powder, onion powder and salt.
2. Place corn chips in an individual serving-size bowl and top with shredded lettuce, beans and chopped vegetables. Finish it off with Cheeze Sauce and enjoy and quick and simple meal!

Stephanie's Suggestions
- We enjoy this meal on nights where we want to be more relaxed and have minimal preparation and cleanup.
- Most corn chips are gluten free but there are some brands that are adding more "healthful" ingredients to their corn chips that do contain gluten so be sure to read the labels carefully.
- If you prefer to use a chip other than corn, simply take a gluten free rice tortilla, cut it with a pizza cutter into 8-12 wedges and bake it in a 375*F oven for 6-7 minutes, watching carefully so as to not burn them.

Savory Coconut Edamame

Edamame, pronounced "ed-ah-maam-eh", are simply immature soybeans in the pod. Edamame are rich in protein, fibre and an assortment of vitamins and minerals.

Makes 6 servings

- 3-4 Tbsp coconut oil (scented variety)
- 1 large onion, chopped
- 2-3 cups shelled Edamame
- 3-4 cups frozen peas
- 1 can lima beans, drained and rinsed
- ¼-1/3 cup chopped fresh basil or 1-2 Tbsp dried basil
- 2-3 tsp vegetable salt or to taste

- Melt 3-4 Tbsp coconut oil in a frying pan over medium heat. Chop onion and sauté in oil for 4-5 minutes or until clear.
- Add edamame, frozen peas and lima beans. Mix together with generous amounts of basil and vegetable salt.
- Serve hot or cold.

Stephanie's Suggestions

- You can find either shelled edamame or ones with the pods still on them. They are usually found in the freezer section of the grocery store. The pods are inedible, however, so be sure to remove them after steaming before using the beans.
- This is a great way to get your kids to eat lima beans! They just love this recipe!

Very Veggie Chili

This chili recipe doubles or triples well and freezing leftovers is a cinch. Heat up leftovers in a crockpot for a meal that takes seconds to prepare. Cook once, eat twice (or three or four times!).

Makes 10 servings

- 3 cloves garlic, minced
- 1 cup chopped onion
- 1 cup diced carrots
- 1 green pepper, chopped
- 1 red pepper, chopped
- 1 28-oz can diced tomatoes with juice
- 1 can black beans or white kidney beans, reserving liquid or ½-3/4 cup dried
- 1 can kidney beans, reserving liquid or ½-3/4 cup dried
- 1 can pinto beans, reserving liquid or ½-3/4 cup dried
- 2 cups whole kernel corn
- 1-2 cans sliced mushrooms or 2 cups sliced fresh mushrooms
- 2 Tbsp chili powder substitute *(See Miscellaneous)*
- 1 Tbsp cumin
- 1 Tbsp dried oregano
- ½ Tbsp dried basil
- ½ Tbsp garlic powder
- ½ Tbsp salt

1. If using dried beans, soak overnight or use quick-soak method found in the "Miscellaneous" section. Cook beans in pressure cooker according to pressure chart on the same page (they can all be combined together as the beans listed in this recipe all take the same amount of time to cook). RESERVE LIQUID. Alternatively, you can use canned beans and reserve the liquid.

2. Cook garlic, onions and carrots in a small amount of water in a large pot until tender. Add the peppers and chili powder. Continue cooking until peppers are tender, about 5 minutes.
3. Add tomatoes, cooked beans with liquid, mushrooms and corn. Add remaining seasonings and stir well to combine.
4. Bring to a boil, reduce heat to medium, cover and cook for 30-40 minutes, stirring occasionally.

Stephanie's Suggestions

- For a special treat, we like to turn this into "Chili Fries" – we top oven baked fries with chili, Cheeze Sauce and sliced green onions. Delicious!

"When flesh food is discarded, its place should be supplied with a variety of grains, nuts, vegetables, and fruits that will be both nourishing and appetizing." Ministry of Healing

Spicy Chickpea and Potato Curry

Our family loves curries and this is one that I make often. For a richer curry, use premium coconut milk or coconut cream and for a thinner sauce, use "light" coconut milk. Either way, it's delicious. Serve over brown basmati rice for a wonderful Thai-inspired meal.

Makes 6 servings

- 4 potatoes, peeled and cubed
- 1 medium onion, diced
- 3 cloves garlic, minced
- 1 large red pepper, diced
- 1 can chickpeas, drained and rinsed or 2 cups cooked chickpeas
- 2 cups frozen peas
- 1 1-inch piece of fresh ginger root, peeled and grated, optional (do NOT substitute with powdered ginger)
- 2 or 3 diced tomatoes (Roma are best but other tomatoes will work well too) OR 1-14 oz can diced tomatoes, drained
- 2 tsp ground cumin
- ¼-1/2 tsp cayenne pepper (or less depending on how spicy you like your food)
- 4 tsp curry powder substitute *(See Miscellaneous)*
- 3-4 Tbsp gluten free soy sauce
- 1 can coconut milk or cream

1. Place potatoes in a pot and cover with water. Cover and bring to a boil over high heat. Reduce heat to medium low and cook, covered, until potatoes are just tender, about 12 minutes. Drain and set aside in another bowl.
2. While potatoes are cooking, heat a large skillet over medium-high heat. Sautee onion, garlic and red pepper in a little water until tender,

about 5 minutes. Add cumin, cayenne pepper, curry powder, optional ginger and soy sauce. Cook for a couple more minutes.

3. Add the tomatoes, chick peas, peas, potatoes and coconut milk. Simmer for 10-15 minutes to allow flavors to meld together. Serve over brown basmati, jasmine or long grain rice. Add additional soy sauce to taste.

Quinoa and Black Beans

Quinoa, pronounced "keen-wah" is a gluten free grain from South America and is a great source of complete protein. It has a light, fluffy texture when cooked and has a mild, slightly nutty flavour. Quinoa also makes a great gluten free alternative to couscous.

Makes 6-8 servings

- 1 medium onion, chopped
- 3 cloves garlic, minced
- ¾ cup quinoa, uncooked
- 1 ½ cups water mixed with 1 Tbsp Chicken-style seasoning *(See Miscellaneous)*
- 1 tsp ground cumin
- Pinch of cayenne
- Salt to taste
- 2 cups corn kernels, frozen or canned
- 2 cups cooked black beans or 1 can, drained and rinsed
- 1 Tbsp dried cilantro or ¼ cup fresh cilantro, chopped, optional

1. Sautee the onion and garlic in a saucepan using a small amount of water. Cook until slightly soft, approximately 5 minutes.
2. Add quinoa, broth, cumin, optional cayenne and salt. Stir well. Bring to a boil over medium-high heat. Reduce heat to simmer, cover pot and cook for 20 minutes.
3. Add corn and black beans and cook for 3-5 minutes or until heated through. Add cilantro and gently stir to combine.

Stephanie's Suggestions
- When cooking quinoa, use the same method as you would for white rice – 1 part quinoa to 2 parts water; bring to a boil and cook, covered for 20 minutes.

- This makes a great meal when paired with gluten free corn muffins and a tossed salad
- I make this often to bring to potlucks and it is well received by everyone – even those not following a plant-based diet!

Fried Rice

If you're pressed for time, this is a great recipe that requires little preparation. It tastes even better the next day so it's the perfect meal to prepare ahead of time and then simply reheat when it's time for dinner.

Makes 6 servings

- 1 recipe Scrambled Tofu made with onion, garlic and peppers *(See Breakfasts)*
- 4 cups hot cooked brown rice
- 1 can mushrooms, drained
- 4-5 Tbsp gluten free soy sauce

1. Cook brown rice according to package directions. You will need approximately 1 ½ cups of uncooked rice to give you 4 cups of cooked rice.
2. Prepare Scrambled Tofu in a large skillet according to recipe directions.
3. Add hot brown rice to cooked tofu. Add mushrooms and gluten free soy sauce. Stir well to combine.
4. Can be used as a side dish or a main dish.

Chickpea and Spinach Pasta

With more and more varieties of gluten free pasta becoming available, it's easier to enjoy delicious meals like this one. You can choose between rice, corn, quinoa, or buckwheat pasta – just to name a few! Grab your favorite kind and make this delicious skillet meal that your family will love.

Makes 4-6 servings

- 1 pound gluten free shell or corkscrew pasta, uncooked
- 1 10-oz pkg frozen chopped spinach, thawed and squeezed to remove water
- 2-4 Tbsp olive oil
- 1 Tbsp Italian seasoning
- 7 cloves garlic, minced
- ½ tsp red pepper flakes, optional
- 1-1 ½ tsp vegetable salt or sea salt
- 1 Red pepper, chopped
- ½ -1 can sliced black olives
- 1 can chickpeas, drained and rinsed (or 2 cups cooked chickpeas)

1. Bring a large pot of lightly salted water to a boil. Add pasta and cook for 8-10 minutes or until pasta is al dente. Drain, rinse and reserve.
2. Heat oil in a large skillet over medium heat. Add garlic, red peppers and red pepper flakes.
3. Sauté for 5 minutes or until the garlic turns light gold. Add cooked pasta and remaining ingredients. If pasta is dry, add a little more olive oil. Mix well and heat through. Serve hot or cold.

Spaghetti Squash — Southwestern Style!

Great main dish to serve in the fall! Pair it with a delicious soup and salad and you've got a great meal.

Makes 6 large servings

- 3 medium spaghetti squash, halved and seeded
- 1 can black beans, rinsed and drained or 2 cups cooked black beans
- 1 green pepper, chopped
- 1 red pepper, chopped
- 2 cups whole kernel corn, fresh or frozen
- 500-mL jar salsa
- 2 cloves garlic, minced
- ¼ cup chopped fresh cilantro or 2 Tbsp dried
- 1 Tbsp chili powder substitute *(See Miscellaneous)*
- 1 tsp salt

1. Preheat oven to 425*F. Place squash halves cut side down on parchment paper. Bake in preheated oven until soft, approximately 1hour.
2. Cool slightly and scrape flesh of squash, using a fork to create spaghetti-like strands. Place in a large serving bowl.
3. Cook peppers and garlic in a little water in a large skillet over medium heat. Once soft, add black beans, corn and chili powder substitute and cook until the liquid has been reduced.
4. Add bean mixture to squash. Add cilantro and salsa. Toss to combine. Season with salt and serve.

Desserts

No-Bake Carob Oatmeal Cookies

Do you remember the classic "No Bake" Oatmeal Chocolate drop cookies? This is them – only better!

Contains Oats

Makes 25-35

- 1/3 cup pure maple syrup
- 1/3 cup honey
- ¼ cup coconut oil, scented or unscented
- 5 tablespoons carob powder
- ½ tsp cardamom
- ½ tsp coriander
- ½ cup peanut butter (or other nut butter of your choice)
- 1 cup wheat free quick rolled oats
- 1 cup shredded, unsweetened coconut
- 1 tsp pure vanilla extract

1. In a saucepan over medium heat and using a whisk, combine maple syrup, coconut oil, carob powder, coriander, and cardamom. Boil for 3 minutes, stirring constantly.
2. Remove from heat and stir in peanut butter, oats, coconut and vanilla until well blended.
3. Drop by teaspoonfuls onto parchment paper lined cookie sheet and chill to set, about 30 minutes.   Store in an airtight container in the refrigerator.

Stephanie's Suggestions

- Carob is a wonderful alternative to chocolate! Not only does chocolate quite often contain dairy products, it's also full of caffeine which is a powerful stimulant. Carob is naturally sweeter than cocoa, is high in calcium and is rich in vitamins and minerals. It can be used successfully to replace cocoa in most recipes. If you're looking for a taste similar to chocolate but without the stimulating effects, carob is a great choice.

Banana Coconut Ice Cream

I never cared much for ice cream.....until I tried coconut milk ice cream! Try it for yourself and see what you've been missing all this time!

Makes 4-5 servings

- 1-400 mL can full-fat coconut cream
- 3-4 bananas, peeled, cut in chunks and frozen for several hours or overnight
- 1 tsp coconut extract
- 1 tsp pure vanilla extract

1. Beforehand, peel and cut bananas into ½ inch chunks. Freeze until solid for a few hours or overnight.
2. Place all ingredients into a blender and blend until smooth. Pour into frozen ice cream maker drum and churn for 15-20 minutes or until desired consistency.

Stephanie's Suggestions
- Using bananas that are as ripe as possible will give you a sweeter ice cream. If you prefer your ice cream a little sweeter, add some honey or maple syrup to the blender just before mixing.
- If you don't have an ice cream maker, you can still whip up this delicious treat. Just use the food processor and make sure all your ingredients are thoroughly chilled beforehand. The finished product won't be quite the same but it will still be delicious nonetheless!

Maple Walnut Ice Cream

A traditional favorite – made healthy! No refined sugar in this recipe – only sweet maple syrup combined with crunchy walnuts and rich coconut cream.

Makes 4 servings

- 1-400 mL can full-fat coconut cream
- 3-4 bananas, cut in chunks and frozen for several hours or overnight
- 1/3 cup pure maple syrup
- ½ tsp maple extract
- 1 tsp pure vanilla extract
- ½ cup walnuts

1 Beforehand, peel and cut bananas into ½ inch chunks. Freeze until solid for a few hours or overnight.
2 Place all ingredients, except walnuts, into a blender and blend until smooth. Add walnuts and pulse a few times to break walnuts into smaller pieces. Pour into frozen ice cream maker drum and churn for 15-20 minutes or until it reaches desired consistency.

Stephanie's Suggestions
- While it's not good to have a diet high in fats and oils, coconut milk is a healthy fat that can be enjoyed from time to time. Coconut milk has been found to stimulate metabolism and it also helps balance blood sugar levels by preventing insulin spikes. Some of the fatty acids in coconut milk can also enhance immune function so take some time to enjoy a yummy treat from time to time!

Candy Cane Ice Cream

One of our favorites! You definitely need the full-fat coconut milk here. Trust me - it's worth it!

Makes 6 servings

- 2-400 mL cans full-fat coconut cream (sometimes called Premium Coconut Milk rather than cream)
- ½ cup maple syrup
- 1 tsp mint extract
- 1/3 cup carob chips

1. Ahead of time, chill the coconut milk for at least 12 hours in the refrigerator.
2. Combine the chilled coconut milk, maple syrup and mint extract in a blender. Process until well combined. Add carob chips and using pulse function, pulse one or two times, just enough to combine the carob chips without chopping them.
3. Chill this mixture if time permits.
4. Pour into frozen ice cream maker drum and churn for 15-20 minutes or until desired consistency is achieved.

Stephanie's Suggestions
- It's important to chill the coconut milk ahead of time because, unlike fruit ice creams, there is no "frozen" component to help speed the chilling process in the ice cream maker.
- An ice cream maker is definitely beneficial in making coconut milk ice creams. You can also blend the ingredients and use it straight out of the blender but the consistency will be much softer.
- Coconut milk ice cream is best eaten fresh. If you try to freeze it, it turns into one solid brick which makes it very difficult to scoop out!

Pecan Pie Crust

Non-pastry crusts like this one are great gluten free alternatives to a traditional rolled-out flaky pie crust. It is also very simple to make and has only a few ingredients.

Makes 1-9" pie crust

- 1 ½ cups pecan pieces
- 3 Tbsp melted coconut oil (this can be warmed over a bowl of hot water)
- ¼ tsp coconut extract, optional (if using scented coconut oil, omit this)
- 2 Tbsp brown sugar or other sweetener of your choice

1. Measure pecan pieces into a food processor that has been fitted with the "S" blade. Pulse several times or until the largest pieces are the size of lentils.
2. While food processor is running, add remaining ingredients. Process until evenly mixed.
3. Pour into a 9" pie plate, spread around and up the sides and press down with fingers.
4. Use in any baked pie recipe.

Vanilla Cupcakes

The first time I tried these cupcakes was at my brother and sister-in-law's wedding. They had a wonderful selection of gluten free and vegan food choices (a dream for someone with food restrictions!). I've made a few changes to the recipe but no changes to the fact that they're delicious! For anyone who has a child suffering from a gluten, dairy, egg, or nut allergy, these make a wonderful treat for a birthday or other special occasion.

Makes 18 cupcakes

- 1 cup + 2 Tbsp sorghum flour
- ¾ cup sifted coconut flour
- 1 cup + 2 Tbsp tapioca starch
- 1 cup cane sugar or coconut sugar (white sugar is fine too, it's just a lot more processed)
- ½ tsp salt
- 1 ½ tsp gluten free baking powder
- 1 ½ tsp gluten free baking soda
- 1 ½ tsp xanthan gum
- ¾ cup coconut milk
- ½ Tbsp lemon juice
- 1 ½ cups warm water
- ¼ cup coconut oil, melted over a bowl of warm water
- 1 ½ Tbsp pure vanilla extract
- Scant ½ cup unsweetened applesauce

1. Preheat oven to 375*F. Pour coconut milk into 4 cup measuring cup. Add lemon juice and set aside.
2. Meanwhile, grease muffin tins. Alternatively, you can line with cupcake papers but be forewarned that any kind of baking that is done without eggs tends to stick to muffin papers. If you prefer decorative

cupcake papers, try spraying the liners after you've put them in the tins.

3. In a large bowl, mix together dry ingredients.

4. Add warm water, coconut oil, vanilla and applesauce to coconut milk mixture. Mix well and add to dry ingredients.

5. Mix with electric mixer on medium-high until smooth. A large countertop mixer works best for this but a handheld mixer will do fine as well. The batter is thick so you will just have to watch it carefully when mixing.

6. Scoop into sprayed muffin tins and bake in preheated oven for 15-20 minutes or until light brown on top and cake tester comes out clean.

Stephanie's Suggestions

- There are many ways to top a cupcake! For a sugar free option, try naturally sweetened jams or make a reduced recipe of Carob Fudgesicles and use as a pudding frosting

- A more traditional buttercream recipe is nice as well. To make a dairy-free version, simply mix ½ cup vegan non-hydrogenated margarine with ½ cup vegetable shortening. Add 1 tsp vanilla or other extract of your choice, 4 cups icing sugar and enough soy or other non-dairy milk to get it to the desired consistency (usually only a couple of Tablespoons at most). Mix in some coloring paste or natural food coloring such as beet juice, if desired, and add gluten free sprinkles or colored sugar of your choice. Cute and fun cupcakes that any child (or adult!) will love!

Coconut Cream Pie

Prepare to indulge yourself! This classic pie is made with no eggs, dairy or gluten so feel free to enjoy this delicious dessert. It's perfect to have on special occasions, to bring to a potluck or to give as a housewarming present. Just be prepared to have everyone ask you for the recipe!

Makes 1-9" pie

- 1-400 mL can coconut milk
- 1-400 mL can premium coconut milk OR coconut cream
- 3 Tbsp gluten free, vegan custard powder (available at most grocery stores)
- ½-2/3 cup white sugar
- Scant ½ cup cornstarch
- ¼ tsp salt
- 1 cup flaked coconut, slightly toasted, divided
- 1 tsp coconut extract
- 9 inch gluten free pie crust, baked OR 1 ½ cups coconut mixed with 3 Tbsp water and 3 Tbsp cornstarch; place in glass pie plate and bake at 375*F for 10-12 minutes
- 1 small container non-dairy whipped topping (i.e. Nutriwhip)
- ½ tsp coconut extract (additional amount)

1. Toast 1 cup coconut by spreading it on an ungreased pan and baking in a 350*F oven for 3-5 minutes, stirring occasionally. Watch carefully as it will burn very easily Reserve 3 Tbsp and set aside for topping.

2. In a medium saucepan, combine coconut milk, coconut cream, custard powder, sugar, cornstarch and salt. Using a whisk, stir constantly and bring to a boil over medium heat. Remove from heat and stir in ¾ cup coconut and 1 tsp of the coconut extract. Pour into prebaked pie crust and chill for 2-4 hours or overnight.
3. Top with non-dairy whipped topping that has been whipped with the ½ tsp coconut extract and reserved toasted coconut.

Stephanie's Suggestions

- To make this into Banana Cream Pie, omit the toasted coconut, substitute banana extract for the coconut extracts and layer sliced bananas on top of the crust before pouring filling in.

Pumpkin Pie

It is said that in early Colonial times, Colonists would slice the tops of off pumpkins, remove the seeds and fill the hollowed out pumpkin with milk, spices and honey. The pumpkin was then baked in hot ashes until done to perfection.   This classic pie is still served using similar ingredients – minus the hot ashes!

Makes 1 pie

- 2/3 cup dates, soaked in water for 3-4 hours
- ¼ cup honey
- 1 cup soy, almond or other non-dairy milk
- ½ tsp cardamom
- ½ tsp coriander
- ¼ cup cornstarch
- 2 tsp pure vanilla extract
- 2 cups or 1 large can cooked, pureed pumpkin (not pumpkin pie filling)
- Pinch of salt
- 1-9" unbaked Pecan Crust *(See Desserts)* or 9" unbaked gluten free pastry crust
- Non-dairy whipped topping, optional

1. Place dates in bowl and cover with water. Let soak for 3-4 hours.
2. Preheat oven to 325*F.
3. Once dates have soaked, drain water and place dates and all remaining ingredients into a blender. Blend until smooth.
4. Pour into unbaked Pecan Crust or gluten free pastry crust.
5. Bake in preheated oven for 1 hour. Let cool and top with gluten free, non-dairy whipped topping of your choice.

Stephanie's Suggestions

- Some interesting pumpkin facts:
    - Did you know that pumpkin flowers are edible?
    - Pumpkins were once the suggested remedy for snakebites and for removing freckles.
    - Pumpkins contain potassium and Vitamin A
    - The largest pumpkin ever grown weighed 1140 pounds
    - Pumpkins are 90% water

Frozen Carob Peanut Butter Pie

This recipe will wow everyone who indulges in this delicious, creamy pie.

Makes 1 pie

- 1 ½ cups water
- 2 cups carob chips
- ½ cup soy milk powder
- 1 tsp vanilla
- ¾ cup smooth, natural peanut butter (non-hydrogenated and unsweetened)
- 1 prebaked gluten free pie crust, 9" or 10" OR 1 ½ cups ground granola mixed with 3 Tbsp oil; mix together and press into pie plate. Bake crust at 375*F for 10 minutes.

1. Blend all ingredients, except peanut butter, in a blender until smooth.
2. Add peanut butter and continue to blend. Pour into prebaked pie shell of your choice and freeze for 4-6 hours or overnight.
3. Take out of freezer 10 minutes before slicing and serving.

Stephanie's Suggestions
- A special thank you to the LifeStyle Matters team for allowing me to include this recipe. For more healthy tips and recipes, visit www.lifestylematters.com.
- Be aware when you are buying carob chips. Some are sweetened with sugar while others are sweetened with barley malt which contains gluten. Check the ingredients carefully before you buy!

Carob Tapioca Pudding

This dessert is an interesting variation on the traditional tapioca pudding – kids love it!

Makes 4 servings

- 3 Tbsp instant tapioca
- 1 Tbsp cornstarch
- Pinch salt
- ¼ cup cane or coconut sugar
- 2 cups almond, soy or rice milk, unsweetened or vanilla
- 1/3 cup carob chips
- 1 tsp pure vanilla extract

1. Whisk tapioca, cornstarch, salt, sugar and almond milk together in a medium saucepan. Let sit for 10 minutes.
2. Add carob chips and bring to a boil over medium heat, stirring often. Remove from heat. Add vanilla and stir well.
3. Pour into bowls and chill.

Carob Toffee Dream Bars

This is one of my husband's favorites – they really are a dream for any sweet tooth!

Makes 9x13 pan

Pastry:

- 2 cups gluten free flour blend
- 2 tsp xanthan gum
- ½ cup brown sugar or Sucanat
- ¼ tsp salt
- ¾ cup non-hydrogenated vegan margarine such as Earth Balance

1. Preheat oven to 350*F. Combine the above ingredients. Press into a greased 9x13 pan. Bake in preheated oven for 10 minutes.

Topping:

- ¼ cup brown rice flour
- 3 Tbsp ground flax mixed with ½ cup warm water; let sit for 10 minutes
- ½ tsp baking powder
- 1 tsp vanilla
- ½ tsp salt
- ¾ cup brown sugar or Sucanat
- 1 cup coconut
- 1 cup raisins, plumped (cover with boiling water, let stand for 5 minutes and drain)
- ¾ cup chopped walnuts
- 1 1/2 cups carob chips

1. Blend flour, baking powder and salt. Beat flax mixture until slightly foamy. Stir the vanilla and sugar into the flax mixture and add to the dry mixture.
2. Spread coconut, raisins, walnuts and carob chips over the base. Pour liquid mixture evenly over top of carob chips.
3. Bake at 350*F for 25-30 minutes. Let cool completely before cutting into bars.

Creamy Carob Fudgesicles

Avocados are an unexpected addition to this pudding/popsicle combination. If you'd like to increase your kids' healthy fat intake, this is a great way to do it!

Makes 8-10 popsicles

- 8-10 dates
- ½ cup water
- 3 medium avocados, pitted and peeled
- 1 can coconut milk
- ¼ cup honey
- 6 Tbsp carob powder
- 2 tsp pure vanilla extract

1. Pour water in blender and place in 8-10 dates. You want the dates to be covered by water so the amount of dates you put in will be determined by how large they are. Pack the dates down if necessary. Let soak for at least 30 minutes.
2. Add remaining ingredients and blend until smooth and creamy. This may take a couple of minutes.
3. Pour into popsicle molds and freeze overnight. Run popsicles under hot water to release them from the molds.

Stephanie's Suggestions
- This recipe can also be used as a delicious carob pudding recipe. Once blended, pour into individual bowls and chill.

Frozen Peanut Butter Fudge

Make sure you allow a few hours for freezing time for this recipe – it's worth the wait though!

Makes 1 - 8" square pan

- ½ cup liquefied coconut oil (scented variety), melted over a pan of hot water
- ½ cup honey
- 1 cup natural, crunchy peanut butter
- ¼-1/2 tsp salt
- ¼ cup carob chips

1. Line 8" square pan with parchment paper.
2. Place all ingredients in a medium bowl. Blend with electric mixer.
3. Pour into pan. Top with carob chips and freeze for 2 hours. Slice and store in a covered container in the freezer.

Stephanie's Suggestions
- This recipe not only works using peanut butter, but any other nut butter will work too – try it with almond butter, sunbutter or soy nut butter.

Maple Apple Crisp

Maple syrup is a delicious natural sweetener that the Lord has provided for us! This healthy sweetener is entirely natural, pure and free from additives or coloring. It also contains high levels of zinc and manganese which keep your heart healthy and boosts your immune system.

Contains Oats

Makes 6 servings

- 5 large apples, peeled, cored and sliced
- ½ cup pure maple syrup
- 1/2 cup rice flour or gluten free flour blend
- 1/2 cup EACH wheat free quick rolled oats and chopped walnuts or pecans
- ¼ cup brown sugar
- Pinch of salt
- 1/4 cup non-hydrogenated vegan margarine, softened

1. Preheat oven to 375*F. Toss apples with syrup and place in a greased 9" square baking dish. In a separate bowl, mix together flour, oats, sugar, salt and nuts. Cut in margarine until mixture is crumbly. Sprinkle mixture evenly over apples.
2. Bake in the preheated oven for 35 minutes, until topping is golden brown. Best served warm.

Stephanie's Suggestions

- White sugar is typically derived from sugar cane which is processed heavily before being sold. Because maple syrup is not processed, it contains higher levels of minerals including calcium, potassium and copper, making it the best sugar alternative available.

- To use maple syrup as a substitute for white or brown sugar, use an equal amount of syrup for the amount of sugar called for in the recipe and reduce the quantity of liquid ingredients (i.e. water, soymilk, etc.) by about ¼ cup.

Miscellaneous

Chicken Style Seasoning

This is a delicious seasoning! Who needs traditional chicken stock that is full of unnecessary salt, additives, preservatives and cholesterol when you have this instead?

- 3 Tbsp sea salt
- ½ cup nutritional yeast flakes
- ½ tsp turmeric
- ½ tsp marjoram
- 1 ¼ tsp garlic powder
- ¼ tsp sage
- ¼ tsp summer or winter savory
- 1 Tbsp onion powder
- 1 Tbsp dried parsley

1. Place all ingredients into blender or grinder. Blend thoroughly and store in a glass mason jar, either in the refrigerator or in a cool, dark place like a pantry.

Stephanie's Suggestions
- Thank you to LifeStyle Matters for allowing me to use this great recipe! www.lifestylematters.com
- This recipe can be used in a variety of ways. Use it to add flavor to soups, rice, beans – anything! It can replace traditional broth in a similar way – 1 Tbsp seasoning in 2-2 ½ cups water.
- The amount of salt in this recipe might seem a little steep, but it's the right amount. If you consider how much the recipe makes and then compare how much salt is in it, it works out to being under ¼ of the bulk. For example, if you're making something that calls for 1 Tbsp chicken-style seasoning, there's only approximately ½ tsp salt in that amount.

Parmesan Cheeze Please!

This is a great substitute for Parmesan Cheese. It goes perfectly on spaghetti and in Caesar salad dressing. Experiment and use it on other things as well and you'll be pleasantly surprised!

- 1 cup sesame seeds
- 1/3 cup nutritional yeast flakes
- 2 tsp onion powder
- 1 tsp garlic powder
- 1 tsp salt

1. Place all ingredients into a bowl and mix thoroughly. Place half of the mixture into an electric coffee mill and grind well. Repeat with the remaining ingredients.
2. Freezes well.

Chili Powder Substitute

You might be surprised to learn that chili powder is actually a mixture of spices and herbs, many of which are irritating to our bodies. This Chili Powder is made from only healthful ingredients that will not leave you reaching for the bottle of antacids.

- ½ cup paprika
- ¼ cup dried parsley
- 1 tsp garlic powder
- 1 ½ Tbsp onion powder
- 1 ½ Tbsp dried basil
- ¼ cup dried oregano
- 1 ½ tsp cumin
- 8 bay leaves, ground

1. Grind bay leaves in a coffee mill or blender. They won't grind powder fine unless you have a high-powered blender so don't worry if there are still small pieces. Add remaining ingredients and blend until combined. Store in a glass mason jar or other airtight container.

Curry Powder

Like chili powder, curry powder is a mixture of various spices and is usually quite hot. This curry powder is much milder but still gives a great curry flavor.

- 1 Tbsp coriander
- 2 tsp cumin
- 2 Tbsp celery seed
- 1 tsp garlic powder
- 1 1/2 Tbsp turmeric
- ½ tsp cardamom
- 1 Tbsp onion powder

1. Mix all ingredients together in a bowl. Store in a glass jar or airtight container.

Fajita Seasoning Mix

Try this homemade seasoning mix the next time your family asks for fajitas. Not only is it much healthier than the store-bought seasoning packets, it's also very cost effective so make a double or triple batch and store it in a mason jar or airtight container so you have lots on hand.

Makes 2/3 cup

- 3 Tbsp cornstarch
- 2 Tbsp chili powder substitute, *(See Miscellaneous)*
- 1 Tbsp salt
- 1 Tbsp paprika
- 1 Tbsp cane sugar
- 1 Tbsp chicken-style seasoning, *(See Miscellaneous)*
- ½ Tbsp onion powder
- 1 tsp garlic powder
- ½-3/4 tsp cayenne pepper
- ¾ tsp cumin

1. Combine all ingredients in a bowl. Store in an airtight container or glass jar.

Flax Egg

A mixture of ground flax seeds and water are a great way to replace eggs in many kinds of recipes. To use this egg substitute, follow these simple directions to replace 1 egg:

- 1 ½ Tbsp ground flax
- ¼ cup warm water

1. Let this sit for approximately 10 minutes or until it's thick and gel-like.
2. This substitute works best for savory things as well as muffins and loaves.

No-Bake Spiced Dough Ornaments

This is a fun craft to make with your children. Just remind them that licking their fingers isn't a good idea!

- 1 cup ground cinnamon
- 1 Tbsp ground cloves
- 1 Tbsp ground ginger
- 1 Tbsp ground nutmeg
- 1 cup applesauce
- 2 Tbsp white craft glue
- A few tablespoons rice flour

1. Combine the cinnamon, cloves, ginger, and nutmeg in a mixing bowl
2. Add the applesauce and glue.
3. Roll the dough out on a lightly floured surface to approximately ¼ inch thickness.
4. Cut with cookie cutters into desired shapes. We cut them into Christmas shapes and make Christmas Tree ornaments with them.
5. Make a hole in the top of each ornament. A drinking straw is a good tool for this job!
6. Bake in a 200* F oven for 1 hour.
7. When they are completely dry and cooled, thread ribbon or string through the hole and tie to secure.

Bean Cooking Chart – Regular and Pressure Cooker Methods

Dried Beans (1 cup)	Soaking Time	Regular Cooking Time	Pressure Cook Time
Adzuki	none	45-50 minutes	15-20 minutes
Black (Turtle)	overnight	45-60 minutes	15-20 minutes
Black-Eyed Peas	overnight	1 hour	10 minutes
Chick Peas	overnight	1 ½-2 ½ hours	20 minutes
Kidney	overnight	1 – 1 ½ hours	10 minutes
Lentil – Red	none	20-30 minutes	5-7 minutes
Lentil – Green	none	30-45 minutes	6-8 minutes
Lima	overnight	60-90 minutes	not recommended
Lima, Baby	overnight	45-50 minutes	not recommended
Mung	overnight	1 – 1 ½ hours	8-10 minutes
Pea, split	none	35-40 minutes	not recommend
Pinto	overnight	1 ½ hours	10 minutes
Soybean	overnight	3 hours	15 minutes
White (Navy)	overnight	45-60 minutes	10 minutes

Bean Quick-Soaking Method:

Instead of soaking beans overnight, use this QUICK SOAK method:

1 Pour desired amount of beans into pot. Cover with water, making sure water level is at least 2-3 inches higher than the amount of beans in your pot.

2 Bring to a boil and boil beans for 2 minutes. Cover, turn off heat, and leave to soak for 2 hours.

3 Once the beans are finished soaking, drain, rinse and cook using the preferred method (either boiling water or pressure cooker) in the Bean Cooking Chart.

The Basics of Sprouting

Sprouting is a technique that has really taken off in the last few years. Although many people are diving into the world of sprouts, many others are still unfamiliar with it and have no idea where to start. I think the most important thing to start with is "why even bother sprouting?" When sprouted, seeds give off more energy in the form of enzymes, vitamins and minerals. Also, during sprouting, the starch is changed to simple sugars, making them very easy to digest. Sprouting increases vitamin content many times over and also develops chlorophyll, an extremely important biomolecule that may aid our health in various ways including, but not limited to, relieving bowel and immune troubles, detoxifying and cleansing our blood, and speeding the healing of wounds.

All these are great reasons to incorporate sprouts into our diets but one of my favorite reasons for sprouting my own seeds instead of just buying them at the store is COST. For the same price, you can buy one small plastic container of alfalfa sprouts (maybe the equivalent of 3-4 cups) OR you can sprout 40-50 cups yourself! Another benefit to doing it yourself is the variety of seeds that you're able to sprout. We've tried alfalfa, buckwheat, lentils, clover, radish, mung beans, chick peas, sunflower, canola, and kelp.

All you need to start sprouting is this:

1. A large mouth mason jar
2. A sprouting screen (available from your local health food store) OR you can use nylon stocking or cheesecloth.

The Method:

1. Soak seeds for 6-12 hours, changing the water once (each package of seeds will give you the recommended soaking time as it varies depending on the type of seed)

2. Drain water from jar through the sprouting screen (or nylon/cheesecloth) top

3. Fill the jar with cold tap water and "rinse" seeds. Drain water through the screen.

4. Turn jar angled downward in a shallow container or on a dish draining rack.

5. Repeat steps 3-5 at least twice per day, more if the weather is hot.

6. Depending on the seeds, sprouting time will vary from 1-7 days. Alfalfa, for example is 5-7 days and lentils are 1-2 days.

I add these delicious sprouts to everything - salads, sandwiches, stir fries - whatever you can think of! And if you are really interested in sprouting, you can get many kinds of specialized sprouting equipment and accessories. Sprouting is really easy and rewarding. Try it for yourself – you'll be very happy that you did!

Sample Breakfast Menus

Breakfast – don't leave home without it!

We've all heard that breakfast is the most important meal of the day – after all, it's "breaking our fast", hence the name "Breakfast". A good breakfast, however, isn't a cup of coffee and a slice of toast as you rush out the door in the morning.

One challenge I've found with gluten free eating is having good breakfast choices that actually fill you up and not leave you hungry an hour later. Yes, it takes a little more time to prepare a filling and nutritious breakfast, but that's a small sacrifice considering how much better you'll feel in the long run! Below are some sample breakfast ideas to give you a great start to your day. Many of the recipes make a lot so you can have them a couple of days in a row which really cuts down on your preparation time. Enjoy!

Day 1:

4-step granola, page 34
Almond milk, page 25
Fresh berries, banana or fresh or canned peaches for granola
Orange or grapefruit
Maple Apple Muffins, page 36
Carob Mint Green Smoothie, page 24

Day 2:

Light and Fluffy Pancakes with diced apples or blueberries, page 30
Orange Tapioca Fruit Salad, page 27
Favorite Fruit Smoothie, page 22
Homemade Trail Mix with almonds, peanuts, raisins, dried blueberries, sunflower seeds and pumpkin seeds

Day 3:

Wheat Free Steel Cut Oats with a drizzle of maple syrup topped with soy, almond or rice milk
Banana
Kiwi
Apple
Creamy Orange Smoothie, page 23

Day 4:

Apple Crisp, page 41
1-2 slices Toasted Honey Molasses Sandwich Bread, page 48
Almond or peanut butter or fruit-sweetened jam
Banana, orange or fresh berries
Dried figs

Day 5:

Julie's Seedy Bars, page 29
Fresh strawberries/blueberries/raspberries
Tangerine or Orange
Gluten free vegan bagel, toasted
Peanut butter or almond butter and honey

Day 6:

Scrambled Tofu, page 42
Potato Patties, page 44
Sliced tomatoes
1-2 slices Toasted Honey Molasses Sandwich Bread, page 48
Nut butter of your choice

Time Saving Tips:

I'll be honest – cooking plant-based, gluten free food takes time. A LOT of time. It's not a simple "hey let's throw a roast in the oven, whip up a package of seasoned rice and add a few rolls from the local bakery" kind of cooking. And it's also not the type of diet where you can just grab a prepackaged meal from the freezer section of the grocery store and pop it in the oven.

One of the major deterrents for people who are considering a plant-based diet is the amount of time that it takes to prepare and cook the food. With everyone's lives seemingly getting busier and busier, many people are finding it hard to cook good, healthy meals. And when you throw in a restriction such as a gluten allergy, it makes it even more challenging.

Below, I've listed a few of my "time saving tips" which will hopefully save you some time in the kitchen.

- Buy reduced, overripe bananas, peel and slice them, put them in a freezer bag and pop them into the freezer. These are great additions to smoothies and coconut milk ice creams and are ready to go at any time. By buying reduced bananas, you not only save a lot of money but they're also at the perfect ripeness for making things sweet.
- Soak beans overnight. Although the "Quick-Soak" method for cooking beans is a handy tool for cooking beans in a hurry, planning ahead and soaking them overnight frees you up during the day to think about other things besides boiling beans.
- When cooking beans, cook a lot more than you need. Separate the extras into 2-cup portions and freeze. When a recipe calls for a can of beans, simply pull out one of your pre-portioned packages of beans and you're all set! This saves time and money.
- Use the same principle above for rice or other foods that freeze well.
- Buy red peppers and mushrooms in bulk. Quite often at our local grocery store, Red Shepherd Peppers come on sale by the case. We buy a couple cases and slice them in the food processor. We then freeze these in large freezer bags where they can easily be added to soups, stir-fries, and Cheeze

Sauce. Mushrooms can be sliced and froze as well and added to spaghetti sauce, chili, scrambled tofu or whatever else you can think of!

- Plan ahead! Although this initially takes some time, it saves time in the long run. Plan at least a week in advance or more if you're able to. This also helps to reduce waste by allowing you to plan your meals around what you're making and what you have on hand so you're not making unnecessary trips to the grocery store to pick up one or two ingredients. You can also plan your meals according to what's on sale at the grocery store.

- Cook once, eat twice. Many recipes are easily doubled. Main dishes such as Lentil Loaf, Pea Soup or Chili can be doubled or tripled and the leftovers can be frozen and pulled out for a quick and easy meal. You're already getting the dishes dirty so why not save time later and just double up on the ingredients?

- Crock Pot cooking is a great way to save time. Even if you're just reheating something like chili or soup but don't want to bother watching it on the stove, throw it into the crock pot and turn it on low for a few hours. Keep in mind that you don't need as much time to reheat a dish as you would to cook it.

- Have the same meals planned for the same day each week. For example, make Tuesdays spaghetti nights and have Haystacks every Friday. This eliminates having to think of what to make on those days and allows you to plan ahead and have certain ingredients on hand. Think of what your family`s favorite meals are and incorporate them into a rotating weekly schedule.

Pantry Check List

These are some of the items that I try to have on hand all the time. I haven't included a whole lot of fresh produce because I know it can be hard to always have fresh items on hand. Also, everyone has their own tastes for fresh produce so add in what you and your family prefer.

- ✓ Almonds, raw
- ✓ Apple juice concentrate, frozen
- ✓ Apples
- ✓ Applesauce, unsweetened
- ✓ Bananas
- ✓ Brown Rice - Short Grain, Long Grain or Basmati
- ✓ Canned peaches
- ✓ Canned tomatoes
- ✓ Canned, sliced black olives
- ✓ Carob chips (gluten free – not barley malt sweetened)
- ✓ Carob powder
- ✓ Carrots
- ✓ Cashews, raw and unsalted
- ✓ Celery
- ✓ Chicken-style seasoning
- ✓ Coconut milk and coconut cream
- ✓ Coconut oil
- ✓ Cold pressed, extra virgin olive oil
- ✓ Dried beans – our favorites are pinto beans, kidney beans, yellow-eyed beans and chick peas
- ✓ Dried herbs and seasonings such as basil, oregano, garlic powder, onion powder, sea salt, dried parsley, paprika, turmeric, thyme, sage, summer savory, dill weed and marjoram
- ✓ Flax seeds
- ✓ Frozen corn

- ✓ Frozen fruit such as bananas, strawberries, blueberries or blackberries (these can be easily added to smoothies or crisps)
- ✓ Frozen mixed vegetables
- ✓ Frozen peas
- ✓ Frozen chopped red peppers (for Cheeze Sauce and stir fries)
- ✓ Garlic
- ✓ Gluten free corn chips
- ✓ Gluten free flours – our favorites are brown rice flour, potato starch, potato flour, sorghum flour, buckwheat flour and tapioca starch/flour
- ✓ Gluten free soy sauce
- ✓ Greens such as spinach, kale or swiss chard (fresh or frozen – either way, it can be added to smoothies and scrambled tofu easily)
- ✓ Honey
- ✓ Instant Tapioca
- ✓ Lemon juice
- ✓ Lentils – French, green and red are the most commonly used
- ✓ Maple syrup
- ✓ Nutritional yeast, flaked
- ✓ Onions
- ✓ Orange juice concentrate, frozen
- ✓ Peanut butter or other nut butters
- ✓ Potatoes
- ✓ Premade gluten free flour blend
- ✓ Pumpkin seeds
- ✓ Quinoa
- ✓ Raisins
- ✓ Split peas
- ✓ Sprouts and sprouting seeds
- ✓ Stevia
- ✓ Sunflower seeds, raw and unsalted
- ✓ Tahini
- ✓ Tofu – Firm, Extra Firm and Silken
- ✓ Tomato paste

- ✓ Unsweetened coconut
- ✓ Vanilla extract, pure
- ✓ Walnuts and/or pecans
- ✓ Wheat free oats
- ✓ Xanthan gum

Resources:

Below is a list of various health-related and gluten-free-friendly resources, books, restaurants and websites that I have found helpful:

- Ministry of Healing
  - Excellent book written on the subject of health and wellness
- Counsels on Diet and Foods
  - Another great book outlining good health as it pertains to our food/dietary habits
- www.lifestylematters.com
  - Great site that includes some recipes, cookbooks and healthy living tips
- www.amazingfacts.org
  - Huge archive of articles, videos and audio programs, many dealing with health-related topics
  - They also have an online bookstore which sells several vegetarian/vegan cookbooks
- Adventist Book Centre
  - Online or visit their store in Oshawa, Ontario. www.adventistbookcentre.com. They also have a mobile store that visits various cities. Call for current bookmobile schedule.
- www.bibleuniverse.com
  - Free online Bible school – or choose to have the free lessons sent to you via the mail. Topics on health are covered.
- http://www.theveggieliciousdietitian.blogspot.ca
  - Bev Miller's blog – full of great healthy living information!
- Wildwood Lifestyle Program
  - http://www.wildwoodhealth.org/lifestyle/
  - Offers health services and 11 or 25 day Lifestyle Programs for anyone seeking to improve their health
- Centurion Ministries
  - Medical Missionary site with information on healthy living

- www.rawnutrition.ca
    - Online source for sprouting seeds, small kitchen appliances such as dehydrators, juicers, sprouters, etc., and a large selection of health resources. Canadian-owned and operated and based out of Otter Lake, Quebec
- www.celiac.ca
    - Canadian Celiac Association
    - Great website with a lot of information for anyone following a gluten free diet
    - Several books are available including an "Acceptability of Foods and Food Ingredients for the Gluten-Free Diet" Pocket Dictionary. This great little book fits into a purse or pocket and is handy when you're in a situation where you're unsure about the safety of certain ingredients
- www.csaceliacs.info/grains_and_flours_glossary.jsp
    - Celiac Sprue Association
    - Grains and flours glossary – large list of flours/grains that are labelled as:
        1. Consistent with a gluten free diet at this time
        2. Questionable due to content, contact or contamination
        3. Not consistent with a gluten free diet at this time
- The Mix Company – www.themixcompany.com
    - This is a great gluten free business out of Eganville, Ontario. It is owned and operated by Randy and Cate Ott who have been in the business for years. They offer a wide selection of gluten free mixes including bread, muffins, cookies, seasoning packets and much more. Many of their mixes are vegetarian/vegan and most can be made that way with a few substitutions.
- Kasha Natural Foods, Pembroke
    - Health food store with lots of options. Offers many gluten free and vegetarian/vegan products.
- Integrated Nutrition, Pembroke
    - Nutrition store with many items to choose from

- Baker Creek Seeds –www.rareseeds.com
  - Excellent heirloom seed company; offers 1400 varieties of seeds for you to grow your own healthy and delicious heirloom vegetables and plants
- The Green Earth Restaurant, Ottawa (100% vegan but not strictly gluten free so be sure to notify your server of any allergies that you have)
- The Green Door Restaurant, Ottawa (not strictly gluten free so be sure to notify your server of any allergies that you have)
- Tea Tree Restaurant, Toronto – all vegetarian with some vegan and gluten free options
- Le Commensal, Toronto – all vegetarian with some vegan and gluten free options
- Crudessence – Montreal – raw and vegan restaurant
- The Magic Oven, Toronto – gluten free and vegan pizza available
- Kelly's Bake Shoppe, Burlington – all vegan and all gluten free
- KindFood, Burlington – all vegan and all gluten free
- The Naked Sprout, Burlington – all vegan, all gluten free and some raw
- Rawlicious, Barrie and Toronto – all vegan, all gluten free and all raw

Index

Notes:

CPSIA information can be obtained
at www.ICGtesting.com
Printed in the USA
LVHW101443280921
698923LV00009B/422